HOME REPAIR AND IMPROVEMENT

HOME SAFETY AND SECURITY

TIME®
LIFE
BOOKS

Other Publications
VOICES OF THE CIVIL WAR
THE TIME-LIFE COMPLETE GARDENER
JOURNEY THROUGH THE MIND AND BODY
WEIGHT WATCHERS® SMART CHOICE RECIPE COLLECTION
TRUE CRIME
THE AMERICAN INDIANS
THE ART OF WOODWORKING
LOST CIVILIZATIONS
ECHOES OF GLORY
THE NEW FACE OF WAR
HOW THINGS WORK
WINGS OF WAR
CREATIVE EVERYDAY COOKING
COLLECTOR'S LIBRARY OF THE UNKNOWN
CLASSICS OF WORLD WAR II
TIME-LIFE LIBRARY OF CURIOUS AND UNUSUAL FACTS
AMERICAN COUNTRY
VOYAGE THROUGH THE UNIVERSE
THE THIRD REICH
MYSTERIES OF THE UNKNOWN
TIME FRAME
FIX IT YOURSELF
FITNESS, HEALTH AND NUTRITION
SUCCESSFUL PARENTING
HEALTHY HOME COOKING
UNDERSTANDING COMPUTERS
LIBRARY OF NATIONS
THE ENCHANTED WORLD
THE KODAK LIBRARY OF CREATIVE PHOTOGRAPHY
GREAT MEALS IN MINUTES
THE CIVIL WAR
PLANET EARTH
COLLECTOR'S LIBRARY OF THE CIVIL WAR
THE EPIC OF FLIGHT
THE GOOD COOK
WORLD WAR II
THE OLD WEST

For information on and a full description
of any of the Time-Life Books series listed above,
please call 1-800-621-7026 or write:
Reader Information
Time-Life Customer Service
P.O. Box C-32068
Richmond, Virginia 23261-2068

HOME REPAIR AND IMPROVEMENT

HOME SAFETY AND SECURITY

BY THE EDITORS OF TIME-LIFE BOOKS, ALEXANDRIA, VIRGINIA

The Consultants

Jeff Palumbo is a registered journeyman carpenter who has a home-building and remodeling business in northern Virginia. His interest in carpentry was sparked by his grandfather, a master carpenter with more than 50 years' experience. Mr. Palumbo teaches in the Fairfax County Adult Education Program.

Mark M. Steele is a professional home inspector in the Washington, D.C., area. He has developed and conducted training programs in home-ownership skills for first-time homeowners. He appears frequently on television and radio as an expert in home repair and consumer topics.

David A. Mandel is the vice president of Liberty Lock and Security, Inc., in Rockville, Maryland. He is a member of the board of directors of the National Burglar and Fire Alarm Association (NBFAA) and a past president of the National Capital Alarm Association.

CONTENTS

Barriers against Break-Ins

A safe and secure home requires protection against fire and accidents as well as burglary. Yet for many homeowners, break-ins remain the principal concern, largely because many residences are poorly equipped to bar intrusion. The improvements on the following pages—a chain-link fence, well-placed yard lights, sturdy locks and window grilles—can provide all the protection most homes need, simply and economically.

A hasp lock →

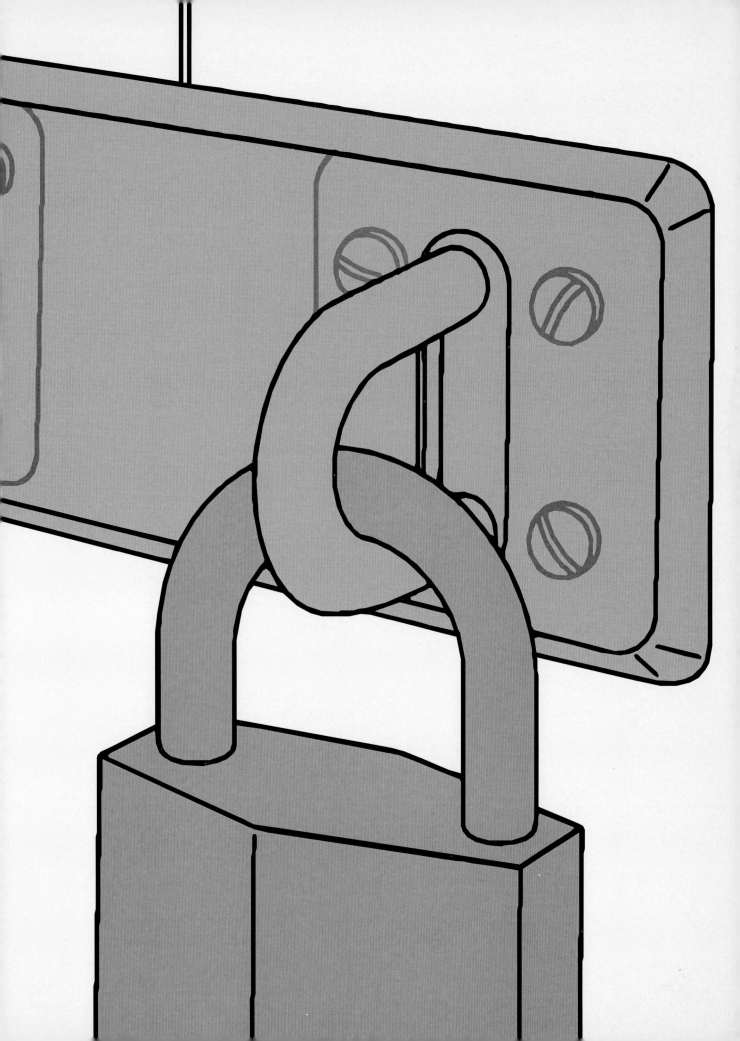

Any fence is a psychological barrier, but a high chain-link fence is a real obstacle to illegal entry. Burglars also know that such a fence makes removal of valuables awkward and highly visible.

Anchors or Concrete: Posts for a chain-link fence must be set in concrete only when the soil is rocky or very sandy. Elsewhere, metal anchors *(right)* simplify the job. They also make the installation go fast: Using anchors, two workers normally can erect 300 to 500 feet of fencing, complete with gates, in a weekend. Concrete footings, on the other hand, require at least 2 days to harden before the mesh can be installed.

Selecting Materials: If you have a choice, buy heavy-gauge posts; lighter ones cost less, but the tops may deform as they are driven into place, complicating the job. Consider cosmetic issues when you choose the chain-link mesh. The least expensive and most common

is galvanized to prevent rust, and it weathers to a dull gray. At additional cost, you can buy mesh and posts with a colored vinyl coating; dark green is popular because it blends with shrubbery.

Planning the Job: Where you can place a fence and how high it is allowed to be are generally regulated by code. It is wise to set a fence a foot or so inside your property line to avoid accidentally infringing on the next lot.

Before ordering materials, draw a rough scale map. Mark the locations of terminal posts—thick posts needed at gates, corners, and other positions as described in Step 1, opposite. Sketch in additional posts, known as line posts, so that no posts are more than 10 feet apart. Using the map, a fence distributor can supply wire mesh, posts, and hardware for the job. Many distributors also rent special tools, such as post drivers, stretcher bars *(page 13),* and cable jacks, or "comealongs," to pull the fencing taut.

TOOLS

Posthole digger
  or shovel
Torpedo level
Post driver
File
Sledgehammer
  (12-lb.)
Hacksaw
Ropes
Lineman's pliers
Cable jacks
Stretcher bars
Hammer
Adjustable wrench
Electric drill with
  carbide bits
Grindstone attach-
  ment

MATERIALS

Wood stakes
Metal post anchors
  or concrete
Line posts and caps
Terminal posts and
  caps
Chain-link mesh
Rail bands and
  cups
Top rails
Tension bars
Tension bands,
  nuts, and bolts
Tie wires
Prefabricated gate,
  hinges, and latch

SAFETY TIPS

Put on goggles whenever you are hammering something at or above waist level, and have your helper don a hard hat to steady posts that you are driving. Gloves protect your hands when you work with individual strands of wire or with wet concrete.

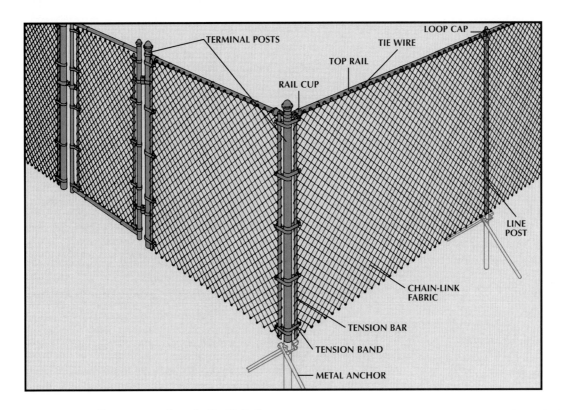

Anatomy of a chain-link fence.
Every component of this fence—the posts, the wire-mesh fabric, and the hardware—is prefabricated. The mesh attaches to heavy-duty terminal posts at corners, ends, and gateways and to lighter line posts between terminals. Both types of posts are set in concrete or secured with metal anchors as shown here. A top rail runs through looped caps on the line posts. Secured to the terminal posts with fittings called rail cups, it provides lateral support. Metal tension bars, slipped through links of mesh and clamped to terminal posts with circular clips called tension bands, hold the mesh taut. Tie wires attach mesh to line posts and top rails.

ANCHORING THE POSTS

1. Digging the postholes.
Some metal anchors require no holes; others are started in holes that are 4 inches deep by 10 inches wide. For concrete footings make holes 12 inches deep by 12 inches wide.
◆ Drive stakes to mark the locations of terminal posts at corners, gates, and fence ends. In locations where the property slopes more than 1 foot in 4 between gates or corners, mark for terminal posts at the top and bottom of each slope.
◆ Have a helper mark the height of the fence on the terminal posts, measuring from the tops *(right)*.
◆ String a line near the ground between the corner and end stakes and mark the line in equal segments of 10 feet or less. Drive a stake at each mark.
◆ At each stake, use a posthole digger or a shovel to dig a posthole appropriate for the anchoring method you have chosen.

FENCE HEIGHT

2. Driving the posts.

◆ Center a terminal post in its hole and, while a helper with a torpedo level holds the post plumb, pound it into the soil with a post driver until the mark on the post is even with the ground *(right)*. Drive all the terminal posts the same way.
◆ String a line 2 inches below the tops of the terminal posts.
◆ Drive the line posts until their tops meet the line.
◆ If the driver deforms the tops of the posts, reshape each one with a file or a grindstone in an electric drill so that a cap will fit.

When a post driver is not available, hold a block of wood over the top of the post as a protective buffer and drive the post with a sledgehammer.

POST DRIVER

HEIGHT MARK

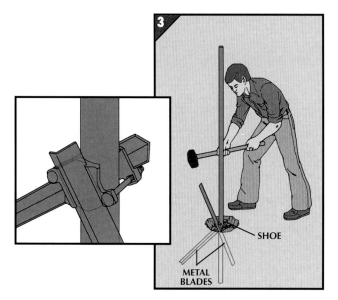

SHOE

METAL BLADES

3. Anchoring the posts.

◆ Bolt a metal anchor shoe loosely to the bottom of the post; orient the slots so that at least one blade will enter the ground at right angles to the fence line.
◆ Insert the metal blades in the shoe slots and drive them into the ground with a 12-pound sledgehammer *(left)*.
◆ Tighten the bolts on the shoe *(inset)*.
◆ In sandy soil, attach a second shoe and drive another set of blades at right angles to the first.

If you dug postholes for concrete instead of for metal anchors, fill around each post with a thick concrete mix. Some professionals overfill the hole slightly, beveling the concrete down from the post so that rain will run off; others underfill the hole somewhat to allow room for soil and grass above the concrete. Let the concrete set for at least 48 hours.

INSTALLING THE TOP RAILS

1. Supports for the rail.

◆ Bolt a pair of rail bands and cups at right angles, 2 inches below the top of a corner post; to set the centers of both cups at the same level, reverse the offsets on the cups *(right)*. Repeat the procedure at other terminal posts.
◆ Slip loop caps over the intervening line posts.
◆ Slide a 20-foot section of top rail through the caps of two line posts and into a rail cup.
◆ Insert additional sections, sliding the crimped end of each section into the end of the preceding one *(inset)* until a section extends beyond the next terminal post along the fence.

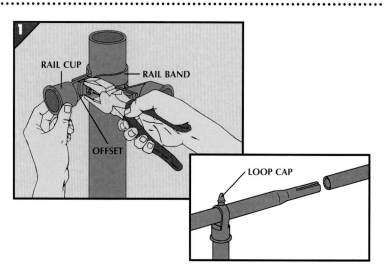

RAIL CUP

RAIL BAND

OFFSET

LOOP CAP

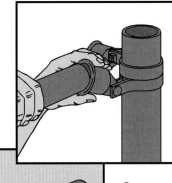

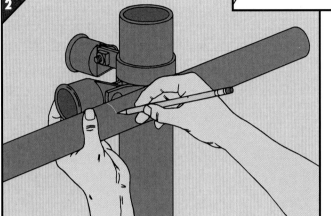

2. Fitting the top rail.

◆ At the terminal post, mark the end of the rail about $\frac{1}{8}$ inch from the inner end of the cup *(left)*, and cut the rail at the mark with a hacksaw.

◆ Turn the cup upward and place the end of the rail against the lower lip of the cup *(inset)*. Then push the rail and the cup downward until they lock together.

HANGING THE WIRE MESH

1. Raising the mesh.

◆ Set a roll of chain-link mesh fabric near a terminal post—an uphill one if the land slopes—and unroll the fabric on the ground outside of the post-and-rail framework.

◆ Tie ropes to the upper edge of the fabric at the end of the roll and at a point 15 feet from the end.

◆ Run the two ropes over the top rail and pull the fabric up against the line posts and the top rail. Secure the fabric temporarily to the top rail with tie wires at intervals of 5 feet.

◆ Continue raising the fabric by the same method until you have reached the next terminal post, then cut the fabric about a foot short of the post.

◆ If a roll ends between terminal posts, splice on a second roll as shown in Step 2; otherwise, proceed to Step 3.

2. Joining two rolls.

◆ Hoist alongside the end of the exhausted roll *(light gray)* one end of a fresh roll *(dark gray)*, following the procedure in Step 1.

◆ Using lineman's pliers, loosen the top and bottom of the end strand, or picket, of the new roll *(near right)*.

◆ Unscrew the picket from the wire weave in a corkscrew fashion.

◆ Pull the ends of the two rolls of fabric together and weave the picket strand back down through the ends of both rolls *(far right)*.

◆ Bend over the ends of the picket strand.

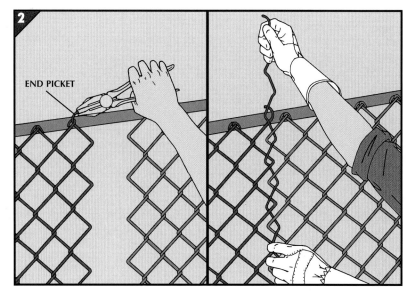

END PICKET

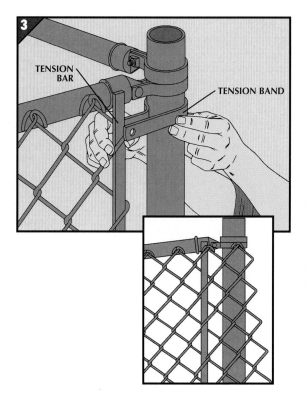

TENSION BAR

TENSION BAND

3. Connecting to a terminal post.

◆ Weave a tension bar down through the row of diamonds nearest the terminal post used as a starting point.

◆ Slip tension bands around the terminal post at $1\frac{1}{2}$-foot intervals, with the flat side of each band on the outside face of the fence *(left)*.

◆ Pull the tension bar between the jaws of the bands, and install bolts and nuts to clamp the jaws shut.

◆ For a section of fence that ends on a slope, have a helper pull the fabric past the terminal post.

◆ Weave the tension bar through the fabric at an angle to keep the bar parallel to the terminal post *(inset)*.

◆ Attach the bar to the post with tension bands, cut off the excess fabric, and bend loose fabric strands around the bar.

TAKING UP THE SLACK

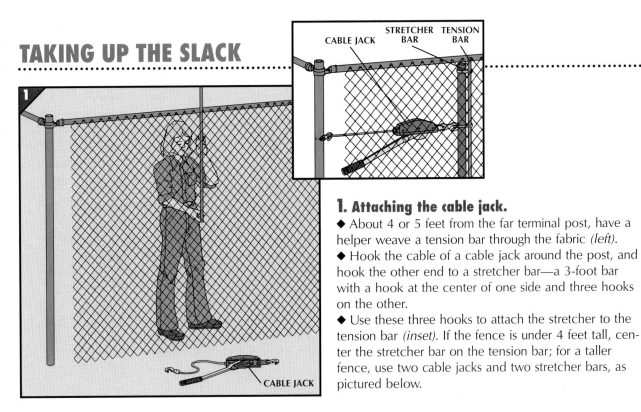

STRETCHER BAR

TENSION BAR

CABLE JACK

CABLE JACK

1. Attaching the cable jack.
◆ About 4 or 5 feet from the far terminal post, have a helper weave a tension bar through the fabric *(left)*.
◆ Hook the cable of a cable jack around the post, and hook the other end to a stretcher bar—a 3-foot bar with a hook at the center of one side and three hooks on the other.
◆ Use these three hooks to attach the stretcher to the tension bar *(inset)*. If the fence is under 4 feet tall, center the stretcher bar on the tension bar; for a taller fence, use two cable jacks and two stretcher bars, as pictured below.

2. Stretching the fabric.
◆ While a helper moves along the fence, lifting the fabric so it clears the ground, work the handles of the cable jacks to pull the fabric taut *(above)*.
◆ Continue stretching the fabric until the rows of its diamond weave are quite straight.

3. Fastening to the far terminal.
◆ Weave a second tension bar into the fabric 4 inches from the terminal post.
◆ Tighten the jacks until the bar is next to the post *(above)*.
◆ Slip tension bands around the post and tension bar and bolt the jaws of the bands together *(Step 3, opposite)*.

◆ Cut off excess fabric with lineman's pliers and release the jacks, then remove the stretcher bars from the tension bar you hooked them to and extract the tension bar.

On land that slopes, align the tension bar at the far terminal post so that it is parallel to it.

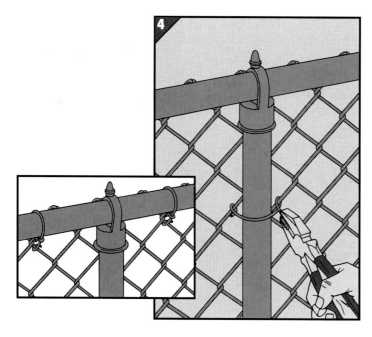

4. Tying down the fabric.

◆ Working inside the fence at each of the line posts, slip the pigtail of a tie wire around a strand of chain link 8 inches below the top rail.

◆ Turn the wire around the post and twist it around a link of chain *(left)*.

◆ Install additional tie wires down the posts at intervals of 12 to 18 inches.

◆ Make a final adjustment of the fabric to set it even with the top rail, and at 2-foot intervals wrap a tie wire around the rail and through the chain link, twisting the pigtail around the mesh and wrapping the other end to the tie wire above the pigtail *(inset)*.

◆ Set terminal post caps on the terminal posts and lightly tap them into place with a hammer.

GATES FOR WALKS AND DRIVEWAYS

Installing gates.

The gatepost side, or leaf, of each hinge has a pin on which the gate turns by way of a hole in the gate frame leaf. Add a single gate as follows:

◆ Loosely bolt the gatepost leaves in their approximate locations with the lower pin pointing up and the upper pin pointing down. Also bolt the other leaves to the gate frame.

◆ With a helper if necessary, fit the gate frame leaves onto the pins and raise or lower both hinges

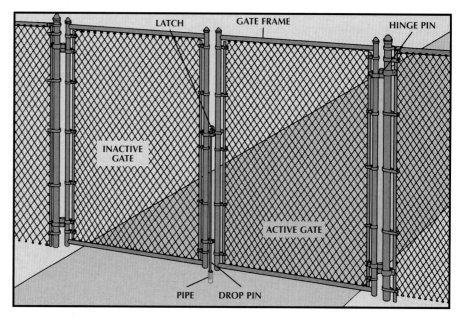

to bring the top of the gate frame even with the top rail. Tighten all the bolts securely.

◆ Bolt a latch to the other gatepost.

◆ For a double gate, use the same techniques to hang both gates. Then bolt the latch to the active gate, close the gates, and let the latch fall.

◆ Loosen the drop pin on the inactive gate and let it drop to the ground. Mark its location.

◆ In a concrete or asphalt walk or driveway, use a carbide bit to drill a hole for the pin; in dirt or gravel, drive a pipe $\frac{1}{2}$ inch wider than the pin to act as a stop.

Low-Cost Lighting

A few well-placed outdoor lights can be highly effective in deterring night prowlers. Just one mercury-vapor lamp mounted on either a utility fixture or a rewired lamppost will illuminate the entire side of a house; incandescent floodlights and low-voltage lights will take care of any remaining dark spots in the yard. Both low-voltage lights and mercury-vapor fixtures for lampposts are sold in kit form, simplifying assembly.

Tapping Power: The handiest power source for new outdoor lights is an existing exterior fixture or receptacle. Otherwise, tap an out- let or junction box in the basement or attic *(page 18)*, making certain that it is part of a 120-volt circuit, not 240 volts.

Nearly any outlet that has two cables entering it contains a suitable power source—a hot supply wire uninterrupted by a switch. A junc- tion box, however, may have only switch-controlled wires. To check, cut off all power at the service pan- el *(page 100)*, then unscrew the wire cap from a connection in the junction box that has at least one black wire. Use a voltage tester to be sure power is off: Hold one probe against the bare wires and the other against a bare copper ground wire. The tester light should not glow. Hold the probes in the same position while a helper re- stores power; if the light now glows, the wire is hot and can serve as a power source.

Protective Armor: Conduit—the electrician's term for pipe—is a fea- ture of virtually any 120-volt outdoor circuit. It must always be used to protect wires aboveground and is often used underground as well. Rigid conduit *(pages 16-17)* is a popular choice because the re- quired burial depth is only 6 inches.

 TOOLS

Voltage tester
Hacksaw
Metal file
Pipe wrenches (10")
Conduit bender

Adjustable wrench (12") or
    open-end wrench ($1\frac{1}{8}$")
Electric drill with masonry
    and spade bits and an
    extender
Cold chisel

Ball-peen hammer
Star drill
Putty knife
Multipurpose electrician's
    pliers
Edging tool

 **MATERIALS**

Cable connector
Wire caps
Box extenders
Metal conduit
Conduit fittings
Conduit straps

Weatherproof
    caulking
Mortar
Green insulated
    wire
Splice caps and
    insulators

SAFETY TIPS *Wear goggles to protect your eyes when hammering a cold chisel or star drill against concrete or masonry.*

A security lighting system.

Although specific requirements can vary widely, the principles of the security light system illus- trated at right can be applied to almost any house. In this situation, a mercury-vapor lamppost fixture illuminates the door, the windows on both sides of the entrance, and most of the front yard. The shadow cast over the garage door and driveway by the retaining wall is eliminated by an incan- descent floodlight aimed down from above. Light from a single mercury-vapor utility fixture bathes both the right side and the back of the house. A streetlight suffices for the left side.

STREETLIGHT

MERCURY-VAPOR
UTILITY FIXTURE

INCANDESCENT
FLOODLIGHT

MERCURY-VAPOR
POST LAMP

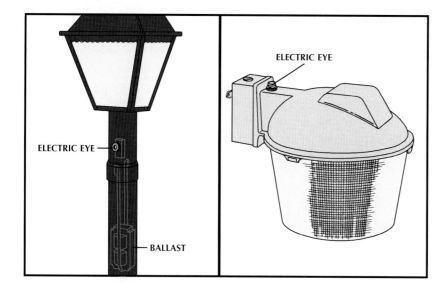

Yard-brightening lamps.

The lamppost fixture at far left has been adapted for mercury-vapor security lighting with two additions: a ballast hanging inside the post and a section of tubing that houses an electric-eye switch. The lamp illuminates a circle about 30 feet in diameter. The 175-watt mercury-vapor utility fixture at near left has a built-in ballast and electric eye. When mounted high above the ground, it lights a circle about 80 feet wide.

Sensor-controlled floodlights.

The motion sensor mounted beneath the fixture at near right and the wand-type electric eye on top of the fixture at far right switch on incandescent spotlights automatically. Both lights can be aimed to shine where needed most. They cast narrow cones of light with a base diameter roughly equal to the height of the fixture above the ground.

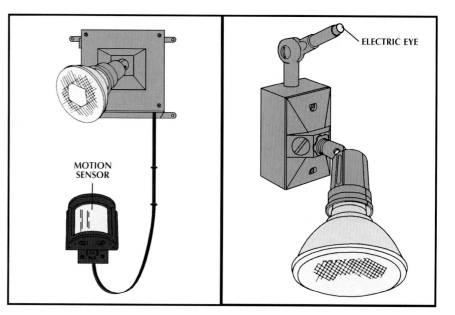

WORKING WITH CONDUIT

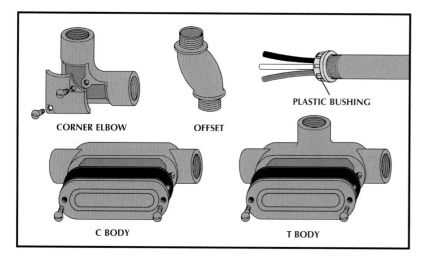

An array of fittings.

At left are the most common fittings for rigid, or heavy-wall, metal conduit. Elbows, for turning corners, have curved access plates that must be weatherproofed with caulking cord. Offsets help jog conduit past small obstacles. Screw-on plastic bushings keep insulation from chafing against conduit edges. The continuous-feed, or C, body provides access to wires in conduit with many turns, while a T body branches a circuit. Both fittings come with weatherproof gaskets.

Buried rigid conduit must be laid at least 6 inches below the surface. If you bury an elbow, C body, or T body, you must mark its location permanently with a fixture or a short stake.

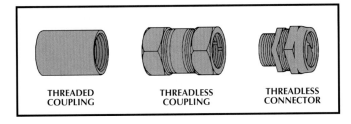

THREADED COUPLING **THREADLESS COUPLING** **THREADLESS CONNECTOR**

Couplings and connectors.

Couplings join two lengths of conduit, and connectors usually serve to fasten conduit to various pieces of hardware. Some used with heavy-wall conduit are shown at left. Threaded couplings, tightened with a pair of 10-inch pipe wrenches, join uncut conduit ends. Threadless couplings join pieces of cut conduit that no longer have threaded ends. After inserting conduit into the coupling, use a 12-inch-long adjustable wrench or a $1\frac{1}{8}$-inch open-end wrench to tighten the nut until the conduit is secure. Threadless connectors join cut conduit to an outlet box, a threaded coupling, or a conduit fitting. Because threadless couplings and connectors are tightened by turning nuts rather than an entire section of conduit, they are also used to join large, unwieldy conduit assemblies.

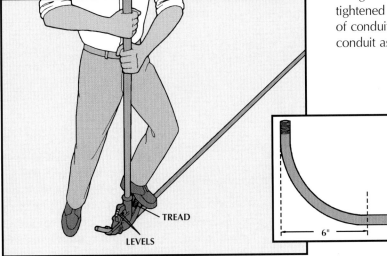

TREAD

LEVELS

6"

Bending metal conduit.

◆ Cut conduit to measure with a hacksaw and deburr the edges with a metal file.
◆ Pencil a mark on the conduit where the bend is to begin.
◆ Insert the conduit into the bender and align the mark with the arrow on the side of the tool.
◆ Step on the rocker tread and pull on the handle *(above)*. To get proper leverage, you may need to brace the opposite end of the conduit against a wall.
◆ Some benders are equipped with 45- and 90-degree levels to indicate when the conduit is bent to the desired angle. Otherwise, use the following rules: For a 45-degree bend, pull the handle until it is vertical; for a 90-degree bend, continue pulling until the handle is halfway to the ground. Either way, the bend will be about 6 inches across *(inset)*.

For an S bend, begin as described above. To make the next part of the curve, turn the bender over so that its handle rests on the ground. Position the conduit in the bender and bend it downward by hand, using a helper if necessary.

RUNNING A CABLE FOR AN OUTSIDE LIGHT

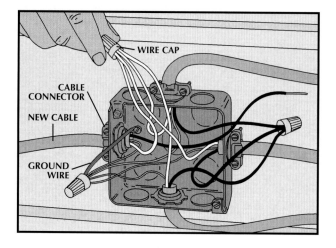

Tapping power.
◆ Turn off power at the service panel.
◆ Remove a circular knockout from the box and install a cable connector in the knockout hole.
◆ Thread a new cable into the box and tighten the connector clamp onto the cable.

◆ Using wire caps large enough to accommodate the extra wire, make the connections—black wire to black, white to white, and the bare copper ground wire to the bare or green wires. Replace the box cover.
◆ Run the new cable to the planned location of the outdoor fixture.

TAPPING AN EXISTING FIXTURE

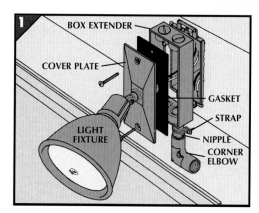

1. Modifying the outlet box.
A fitting called a box extender provides the room needed to make wiring connections and attach conduit.
◆ Turn off the power. Remove the light fixture (or receptacle) from the box. Undo the electrical connections.
◆ Screw one end of a short piece of conduit called a nipple into an elbow and the other end into a conduit hole in the box extender. Temporarily screw the fixture, gasket, cover plate, and extender to the outlet box.
◆ Clamp the nipple to the wall with a conduit strap and caulk any gap between the box extender and the house.
◆ Later, remove the fixture to fish cable into the extender and to make the necessary wire connections, then screw the fixture permanently in place.

2. Assembling conduit along the house.
◆ Run conduit from the elbow at the box extender to the bottom course of siding. Strap the conduit to the wall.
◆ With a conduit bender *(page 17),* shape a conduit section to curve around the bottom of the siding and rest on the floor of the trench. Check the fit of this piece after making each bend.
◆ With a threadless coupling, link the contoured section to the conduit strapped to the house.

INSTALLING A BOX IN CONCRETE BLOCK

1. Making an opening.

You can recess an indoor box with adjustable ears into a block wall.

◆ Hold the box against the center of a block and outline it with tape. If seams between blocks have been stuccoed over, bore a test hole with a masonry bit in an electric drill to find a hollow. Insert a bent wire in the hole, feel around for the sides of the hollow, and mark a box opening between them.

◆ Use a $\frac{3}{8}$-inch electric drill with a $\frac{1}{2}$-inch masonry bit to bore several holes inside the tape. Finish the opening with a cold chisel and ball-peen hammer, making the hole $\frac{1}{4}$ inch wider and longer than the box.

◆ Attach the masonry bit to an extender and drill a single hole through the far side of the block. Hammer a star drill to enlarge the hole for cable.

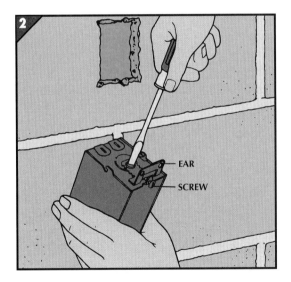

2. Mortaring the box in place.

◆ Insert screws loosely into the box's fixture-mounting screw holes to keep out mortar.

◆ Adjust the ears so that the edge of the box extends about $\frac{1}{16}$ inch from the wall; this slight extension allows the cover-plate gasket to form a tight seal around the box.

◆ Clamp the cable to the box.

◆ Slide the box into place and press mortar into the gap between the box and hole with a putty knife. Mortar must completely fill the gap to anchor the box securely and to weatherproof the installation.

◆ When the mortar has dried, remove the screws from the mounting tabs.

AN EXIT FROM A BASEMENT OR CRAWLSPACE

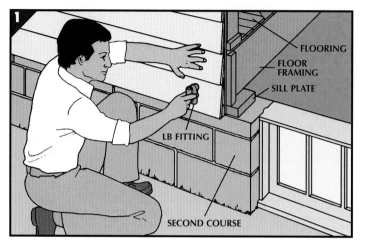

FLOORING
FLOOR FRAMING
SILL PLATE
LB FITTING
SECOND COURSE

1. Drilling the exit hole.

For underground-feeder, or UF, cable, install an L-shaped connector known as an LB fitting; individual wires require an outlet box and a cover without openings.

◆ Locate an exit point above the sill plate where joists will not hinder work and where an LB fitting or outlet box will not overlap a siding joint *(left)*.

◆ Drill a $\frac{1}{8}$-inch test hole through the siding and floor framing behind it. If the exit point is satisfactory, enlarge the hole with a $\frac{7}{8}$-inch spade bit.

In concrete block, bore through the center of a block in the second course below the sill plate. Enlarge the test hole by hammering a $\frac{7}{8}$-inch star drill, rotating the tool an eighth-turn after each tap. Make an identical hole in the other side of the block.

2. Installing the fitting.

◆ Select a nipple long enough to reach through the wall and screw it to an LB fitting or the back of an outlet box.

◆ Temporarily insert the nipple into the hole, and bend conduit *(page 17)* to run from the fitting into the conduit's trench.

◆ Withdraw the fitting from the wall, screw it onto the conduit, and push the nipple back through the wall.

◆ Strap the conduit to the side of the house. If an outlet box is used, screw the box to the wall and caulk around it; for an LB fitting, caulk around the nipple where it enters the house.

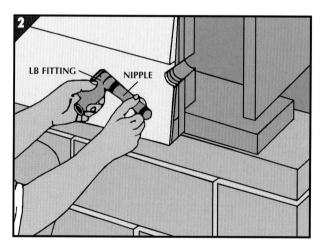

LB FITTING
NIPPLE

RECESSING A LIGHT IN A STAIRWAY WALL

COVER PLATE

NIPPLE — — FIXTURE

Securing the fixture.
◆ With a cold chisel, chip out a brick and the surrounding mortar.
◆ Bore a $\frac{7}{8}$-inch hole through the wall and into the conduit trench with a star drill.
◆ Assemble the fixture as necessary. In the back, screw a nipple long enough to extend into the trench *(left)*. Push the fixture into the recess.
◆ If there is space around the front of the fixture, hammer in wood shims at the top and bottom. Pack mortar around the fixture and the nipple where it protrudes from the back of the wall.
◆ After the mortar dries, screw an outdoor box to the protruding nipple and thread the fixture leads through the nipple and into the box.
◆ Install a light bulb and mount the fixture cover plate.

MOUNTING A FIXTURE IN AN EAVE

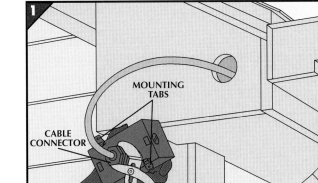

1

MOUNTING TABS

CABLE CONNECTOR

1. Installing a weatherproof outlet box.
◆ Drill a 1-inch exit hole in the house exterior at the location of the new fixture—in this example, in the fascia. Tap an indoor circuit *(page 18)* and run cable through the exit hole.
◆ Outside the house, slide the four pieces of a weatherproof cable connector *(inset)* over the end of the cable and tighten the connector. Hold the connector with pliers and screw an outdoor outlet box onto it.
◆ Set the connector in the hole and screw the box in place through the hinged mounting tabs.

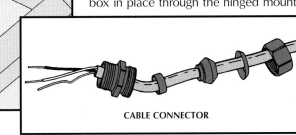

CABLE CONNECTOR

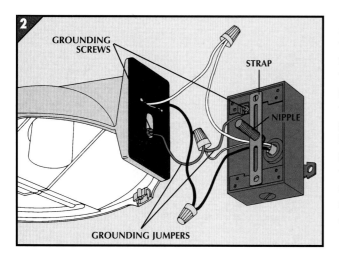

2. Wiring the fixture.

◆ Screw together the threaded nipple and the strap that come with the mercury-vapor lamp fixture, and fasten the strap to the tabs of the outlet box with the screws provided.

◆ Connect one grounding jumper—a 6-inch length of green insulated wire—to the green grounding screw on the back of the fixture, and another to the grounding screw of the outdoor box.

◆ As a helper holds the fixture, use wire caps to connect the jumpers to the bare wire of the cable, and make the connections between the other fixture and cable wires—white to white and black to black.

3. Mounting the lamp.

◆ Slide the metal hood of the fixture over the nipple and screw a cap nut onto the nipple until the hood gasket is tight against the outlet box.

◆ Fit the doughnut-shaped plastic lens to the fixture with the clips provided by the manufacturer, then screw the mercury-vapor bulb into its socket.

◆ To test the lamp, cover the electric eye on top of the hood with black tape and restore power. The lamp should turn on in about 1 minute.

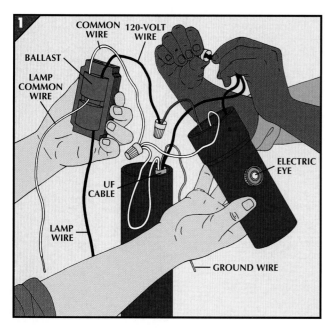

ADAPTING A YARD LIGHT TO A MERCURY-VAPOR BULB

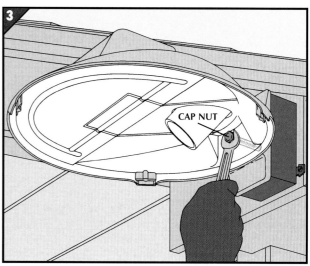

1. Connecting the ballast and electric eye.

◆ Turn the power off. Remove the incandescent fixture from the top of the lamppost and disconnect its wires.

◆ Have a helper hold a ballast matching the wattage of the bulb and an electric eye housed in a length of lamppost tubing while you connect their wires to the cable inside the post. Using wire caps, join the white wires of the cable and the electric eye to the ballast wire marked COMMON, the black cable wire to the black wire of the electric eye, and the red wire of the electric eye to the ballast wire marked 120 VOLTS or LINE. Do not, at this point, connect the wires marked LAMP and LAMP COMMON.

◆ Extend the bare ground wire of the cable with a 1-foot length of green insulated wire.

2. Mounting the ballast and eye.
◆ Set the ballast, with the lamp and lamp common wires up, into the U-shaped strap provided by the manufacturer, lower the strap into the lamppost, and hook the tabs at the ends of the strap over the outside of the post.
◆ Thread the lamp, lamp common, and cable ground wires through the tubing that houses the electric eye. Fit the bottom of the tubing over the top of the lamppost and, using holes in the tubing as a template, drill holes in the post.
◆ Fasten the tubing with the self-tapping screws provided by the manufacturer.

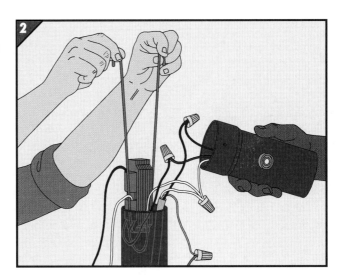

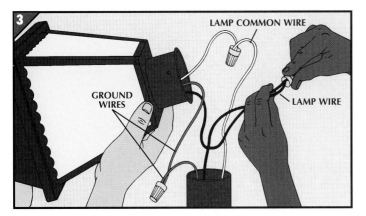

LAMP COMMON WIRE

GROUND WIRES

LAMP WIRE

3. Wiring the lamp fixture.
◆ Have a helper hold the fixture while you make connections with wire caps: the lamp's green or bare ground wire to the green cable wire, the lamp's white wire to the ballast wire marked LAMP COMMON, and the lamp's black wire to the ballast wire marked LAMP.
◆ Slide the fixture over the top of the electric-eye tubing and use the holes in the bottom of the fixture as a template to drill matching holes in the tubing.
◆ Screw the lamp to the tubing.

Install a mercury-vapor bulb that matches the wattage of the ballast and has a "medium base," designed to fit a standard lamp socket. Test the lamp fixture as explained in Step 3, opposite.

AN INCANDESCENT FLOOD LAMP

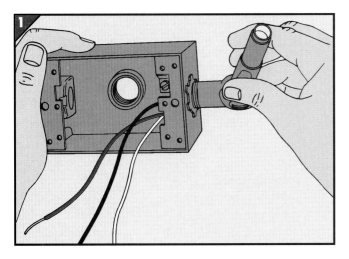

1. Installing the box and electric eye.
◆ Thread the wires of a wand-type electric-eye switch through the hole at one end of an outdoor outlet, screw the switch into the box, and tighten the star nut.
◆ Tap an indoor circuit (page 18) and mount the outlet box as described on pages 21 to 22. Then aim the wand of the electric eye toward the sky and away from streetlights and other sources of light.

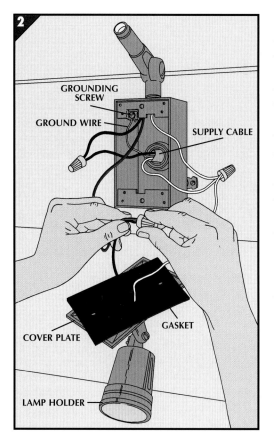

2. Wiring the lamp holder.

◆ Attach a weatherproof lamp holder in the threaded opening in the outlet-box cover and tighten the star nut.

◆ Slide the gasket over the lamp-holder wires and connect the wires with wire caps. Connect the bare ground wire of the supply cable to the grounding screw of the outlet box, join all white wires, connect the black cable wire to the black wire from the electric eye, and connect the eye's red wire to the lamp holder's black wire.

◆ Screw the cover plate to the outlet box, making sure that the gasket seats snugly. Install a weatherproof 75-watt incandescent floodlight, aim the lamp, and test it (page 22, Step 3).

In image 2:
GROUNDING SCREW
GROUND WIRE
SUPPLY CABLE
COVER PLATE
GASKET
LAMP HOLDER

LOW-VOLTAGE LIGHTING

1. Installing the transformer.

◆ Mount the wall bracket supplied with the transformer at least 12 inches above the ground on a wall or post, and within 6 feet of a receptacle; then push the transformer onto the bracket.

◆ Place the fixtures and string the low-voltage cable from the transformer, leaving enough slack to follow walkways and flower beds. Leave 12 inches of additional slack at each fixture.

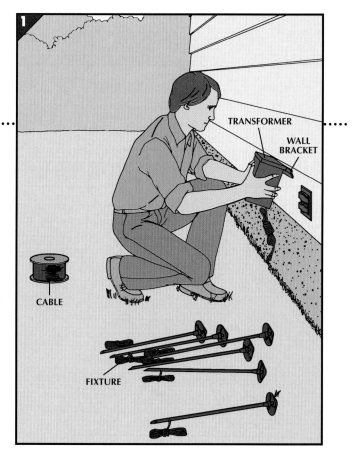

In image 1:
TRANSFORMER
WALL BRACKET
CABLE
FIXTURE

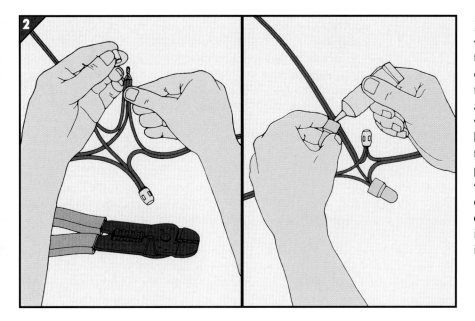

2. Using splice caps.

◆ For a fixture with wire leads, cut the cable at the locations you have chosen, strip $\frac{3}{8}$ inch of insulation from each cable and fixture wire, and twist each fixture wire to the wires from each end of the cut cable. Crimp a splice cap over each three-wire connection with multipurpose electrician's pliers *(far left)*.

◆ Partially fill an insulator with silicone caulking compound and slip it over the splice cap *(near left)*, making sure that the cap is embedded in the compound.

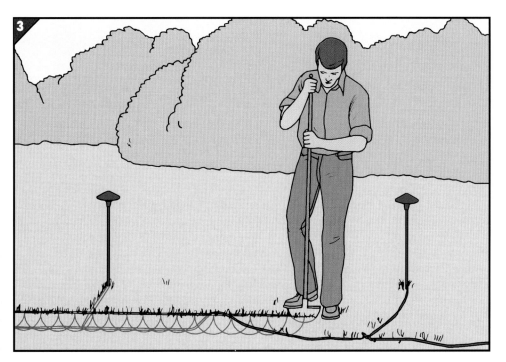

3. Hiding the cable underground.

◆ Push an edging tool into the ground with one foot, rocking it back and forth to exert a downward and sideward pressure. Overlapping strokes will cut a narrow slit.

◆ Tuck the cable into the slit and step along the top to press the turf back together.

Doorway security begins with a metal door or a solid-core wood door. Hollow-core and paneled wood doors are both too weak to offer much protection. A metal door made of steel no thinner than 16 gauge is adequate. In wood doors, a core of laminated 2-by-4s is stronger than a particle board core.

Windows in an exterior door reduce security, as does a mail slot within reach of the latch. To see who is outside, install a viewer (below). Steel rods slipped into the edge of a wood door (page 28, top) help thwart attempts to saw out locks and latches.

A Strong Frame: If your door jambs are made of steel—check them with a magnet—you need do nothing to strengthen them. With wood jambs, however, even the sturdiest door may be installed in ways that make a break-in easy.

To check the door mounting, begin by removing a hinge screw. Replace short screws with 3-inch No. 10 wood screws that extend into the stud behind the jamb. For the best grip between screw and wood, use the hole-drilling method shown at the top of the opposite page.

Unless adequately reinforced at hinges, deadbolts, and latches, many wood jambs can be levered away from the door far enough to free the bolt or latch. To determine whether your doorway has this weakness, remove the interior casing and inspect the spaces immediately outside the jambs. Add plywood filler and shims as necessary (pages 29-30).

Look into the deadbolt hole in the jamb. If you see wood at the bottom, replace the metal frame, or strike, with a heavy-duty strike box (pages 28-29) to encase the bolt in metal.

Special Cases: If your door opens outward, the hinges are outside of the house. It is a simple matter for a burglar to extract the hinge pins and remove the door from the frame. To foil any such attempt, use the technique that is shown at the top of page 31.

Sliding glass doors are especially vulnerable if the movable panel can be lifted out of the lower track. A few screws driven into the upper track solves the problem (page 31, bottom).

 TOOLS

Electric drill
Bell-hanger drill bit (12")
Drill guide
Chisel
Pry bar
Carpenter's nippers
Mallet
Hammer
Hacksaw

 **MATERIALS**

Steel rods ($\frac{1}{4}$" diameter, $7\frac{1}{4}$" long)
Wood screws (3" No. 10)
Scrap plywood
Shims
Common nails (2" and 4")
Finishing nails ($1\frac{1}{2}$" and 2")
Sheet-metal screws ($1\frac{1}{2}$" No. 12)

 **SAFETY TIPS**

Goggles protect your eyes from metal filings when you are hammering nails and drilling overhead.

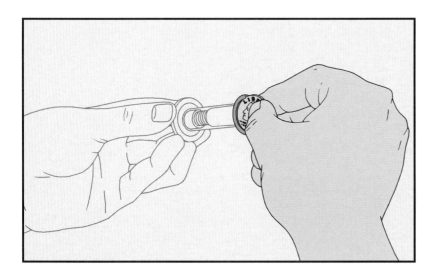

Installing a wide-angle viewer.

To see who is outside without having to open the door, install a viewer. Models with a 180-degree field of view, sometimes called fisheye viewers, make it impossible for a person to duck out of sight.

◆ At eye level in the center of the door, drill a hole as wide as the viewer shank, usually $\frac{1}{2}$ inch.
◆ Insert the two halves of the viewer and screw them together by hand if the interior section is knurled, or with a coin if it is slotted (left).

HOLES TO GRIP SCREWS TIGHT

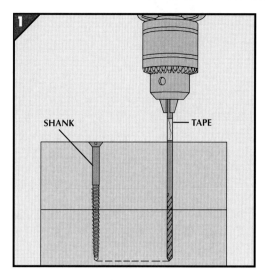

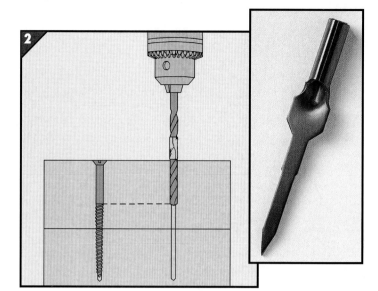

1. The pilot hole.
Screw holes may be drilled with ordinary bits, as shown in these illustrations, or as a single step with a combination bit *(photograph)*.
◆ To use ordinary bits, select a pilot-hole bit from the chart below.
◆ Wrap masking tape around the bit $\frac{1}{16}$ inch farther from the tip than the length of the screw.
◆ Drill as deep as the tape permits.

2. The shank hole.
◆ Select a shank-hole bit from the chart.
◆ Tape the bit to avoid enlarging the pilot hole below the depth of the shank, then drill to the tape.

MATCHING BITS TO SCREWS

Screw Gauge	No. 6	No. 7	No. 8	No. 9	No. 10	No. 12	No. 14
Pilot-hole bit	$\frac{5}{64}$"	$\frac{3}{32}$"	$\frac{3}{32}$"	$\frac{7}{64}$"	$\frac{7}{64}$"	$\frac{1}{8}$"	$\frac{9}{64}$"
Shank-hole bit	$\frac{9}{64}$"	$\frac{5}{32}$"	$\frac{11}{64}$"	$\frac{3}{16}$"	$\frac{13}{64}$"	$\frac{15}{64}$"	$\frac{1}{4}$"
Lengths available	$\frac{3}{8}$" - $1\frac{1}{2}$"	$\frac{1}{2}$" - $1\frac{1}{2}$"	$\frac{1}{2}$" - $1\frac{1}{2}$"	$\frac{3}{4}$" - $2\frac{1}{2}$"	$\frac{3}{4}$" - $3\frac{1}{2}$"	$\frac{3}{4}$" - $3\frac{1}{2}$"	1" - 4"

Bits for pilot holes and shank holes.
This chart specifies the sizes of bits needed to drill pilot holes and shank holes for seven common gauges of wood screw. For sheet-metal screws, drill a pilot hole only. If screws supplied with the hardware are not identified by gauge number, determine their gauge by matching them against the actual-size drawings of screwheads above. If screws supplied with the hardware are too short for secure fastening, use the bottom row of the chart to help you select longer screws of the same gauge.

SAWPROOFING A DOOR

Steel bars for the lock area.

To shield the lock in a solid-core wood door, bore holes into the lock-side edge and insert steel rods.

◆ With a 12-inch-long, $\frac{1}{4}$-inch bell-hanger bit and drilling no closer than 1 inch to the bolt or latch plates, bore five holes above the locks and five holes below them. Space the holes 2 inches apart, and use a drill guide to keep them at a 90-degree angle to the door edge. To make all holes an equal depth, wrap tape $8\frac{1}{2}$ inches from the tip of the bit.

◆ In cases where the door has a dead-bolt, drill as many holes as possible between the deadbolt and the main lock.

◆ Into each hole, tap a $7\frac{1}{2}$-inch length of unthreaded $\frac{1}{4}$-inch steel rod, then seal the holes with wood filler.

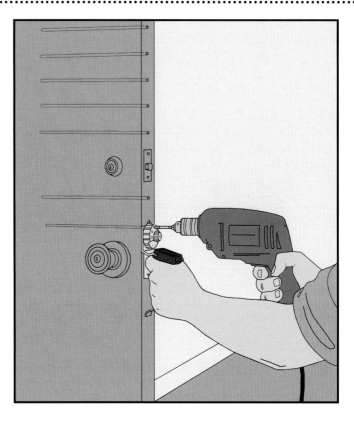

A DEADBOLT STRIKE BOX

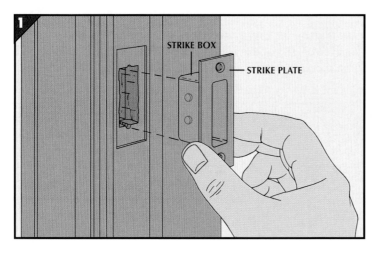

STRIKE BOX

STRIKE PLATE

1. Recessing the strike.

◆ Unscrew the old strike plate and enlarge the opening in the jamb with a chisel to accommodate the new strike box.

◆ Set the box in the jamb periodically as you work to check its position; the bolt of the lock must slide into the box without binding. If necessary, enlarge the opening for a good fit.

◆ Hold the box in the jamb and trace around the strike plate with a pencil.

◆ Chisel a recess, or mortise, within the outline so that the strike plate lies flush with the surface of the wood.

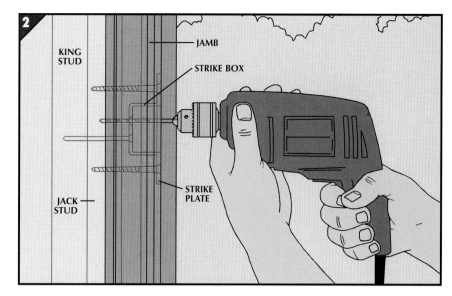

2. Fastening the strike.

With the strike in the jamb, use the screw holes in the strike plate and strike box as guides to bore into the studs beyond the jamb. Drill the holes to fit 3-inch No. 10 wood screws, using the hole dimensions and drilling method shown on page 27.

STIFFENING A FRAME

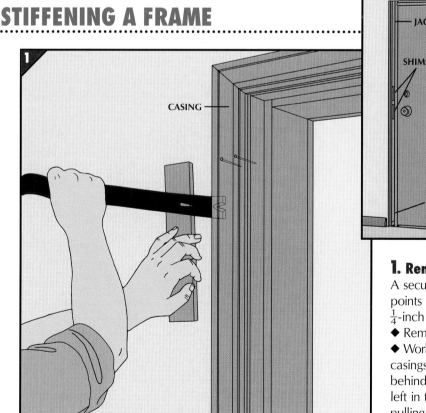

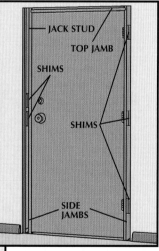

1. Removing the side casing.

A securely braced doorjamb requires, at each of the points indicated in the inset, 4- by 6-inch fillers of $\frac{1}{4}$-inch plywood and two pieces of door shim.
◆ Remove the strikes from the doorjamb.
◆ Working from the bottom up, remove both side casings with a pry bar, using a thin scrap of wood behind the bar to protect the wall *(left)*. Extract nails left in the wall or casings with carpenter's nippers, pulling casing nails through the back of the boards.
◆ Check the space between the jambs and the jack studs. If you find no shims at the locations indicated *(inset)*, proceed to Step 2; if you do, go to Step 3.

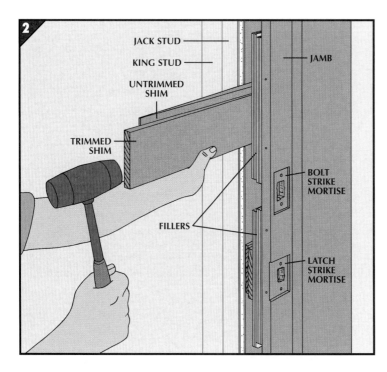

2. Adding shims.

◆ Insert plywood filler behind the jamb, leaving space for the thick end of an untrimmed shim.

◆ Push the shim into the gap between filler and stud, then tap a shim with 3 inches trimmed from its thin end into the opening, thin end first, until the shims are snug. Score and snap off shim ends.

◆ Install one shim assembly behind each hinge; at the deadbolt strike, use two fillers separated by a gap for the box of a high-security strike *(pages 28-29)*.

◆ To secure the fillers, replace short hinge screws with 3-inch No. 10 wood screws and drive pairs of identical screws above and below each strike plate.

3. Reinstalling the casing.

◆ Nail the side casings to the jambs and the jack studs, from top to bottom, using 2-inch finishing nails in the studs and $1\frac{1}{2}$-inch finishing nails in the jambs, reusing old nail holes where feasible.

◆ Secure the side casings to the top casing with one 2-inch nail driven horizontally and another driven vertically into each mitered joint *(right)*.

Pinning exterior hinges.

◆ Where a door swings out instead of in, remove a pair of screws from each hinge—one from the jamb leaf and a second, opposite the first, from the door leaf.
◆ Hammer 4-inch nails into the empty screw holes in the jamb leaves, leaving $\frac{1}{2}$ inch of each nail protruding.
◆ Cut off the nailheads with a hacksaw.

When hanging a new outward-opening door, use security hinges such as the one shown here. It has a metal projection that takes the place of the nail described above. A setscrew prevents the hinge pin from being pried out.

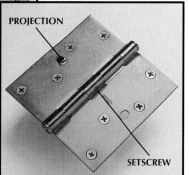

PROJECTION

SETSCREW

Keeping a sliding door in its tracks.

◆ Open the door and drill holes at 10-inch intervals in the overhead track with an $\frac{11}{64}$-inch bit.
◆ Drive a $1\frac{1}{2}$-inch No. 12 sheet-metal screw into each hole, allowing the screwheads to protrude enough to prevent the door from being lifted out of its tracks but not so far that they will rub against the door as it is opened and closed (inset).

Door locks operate on a simple and ancient principle. A rigid locking arm, called a bolt, is mounted in or on the door so that it can be slid into a socket, or strike, attached to the doorframe. Two types of locks are in wide use today: the key-in-knob (also called a spring-latch lock) and the deadbolt.

Key-in-Knob Locks: The locking arm of this type of lock is activated by a spring mechanism and engages automatically as the door is closed. Most key-in-knob locks are not as secure as a deadbolt, since a burglar can pop the latch out of the strike.

Deadbolt Locks: A deadbolt offers better protection because the bolt must be opened and closed manually by a thumb turn or a key. Generally such a lock is installed as a backup to a key-in-knob lock. The simplest kind of deadbolt is a rim lock, which is mounted on the inner face of a door and doorframe; deadbolts that are installed inside a door and lock into a strike box inside the jamb are far stronger.

Some newer key-in-knob designs can be set to function like a deadbolt when extra security is desired. An-other versatile locking system is a mortise lock, which combines a deadbolt and a spring-latch mechanism in a single handsome (and expensive) unit.

For any door containing glass, use a double-cylinder deadbolt—that is, one operated by a key on both sides. This will prevent a burglar from reaching through a broken pane to open the door.

Special Locks: Other locking systems can serve specialized roles in the home. Sliding doors, for instance, can be locked with a metal bar braced between the frame and the sliding panel, or with a lock that pins movable and stationary panels together. Thumb-activated vertical bolts can help secure a pair of French doors. A strong padlock suffices on most garages, and shed doors need only a hasp and padlock.

Choosing and Installing Locks: When buying any kind of keyed lock, ask for the five-pin cylinder type *(below)*. Check the wood screws that come with the lock: Many are too short for secure attachment. Also, keep in mind that even the best lock has little value unless it is installed in a strong door and frame *(pages 26-31)*.

THE INNARDS OF A FIVE-PIN CYLINDER

The lock most widely used today contains sets of pins and springs in two cylinders—a small one, known as the plug, that fits within another, called the shell. The plug and shell have rows of holes—at least five in the best locks—that line up when the bolt or latch is fully locked *(inset, top)*. In each hole of the shell, a spring pushes against two pins—one in the shell atop a second one in the plug—forcing them down so that the shell pin enters the corresponding hole in the plug, preventing that cylinder from turning.

Inserting a notched key lifts both of the pins in each hole *(inset, bottom)* so that the separation between every shell and plug pin coincides with the narrow space—called the shear line—between the plug and the shell. Turning the key causes the plug to rotate, since the shell pins no longer engage it. The plug's action moves the drive bar and activates the latch or bolt.

Such locks have always proved difficult to pick, and refinements to their works have made them even tougher.

One manufacturer, for instance, bevels the pins and the key notches so that the key not only raises the pins but also rotates them; unless each pin is oriented correctly, the plug cannot move.

Some locking systems have no key cylinders. In push-button locks the correct combination of numbered buttons must be depressed before the bolt can be moved. And in a computerized system, a magnetically coded plastic card is inserted in a scanner; if the code is correct, the computer activates an electromagnet in the strike box that retracts a bar to disengage the bolt.

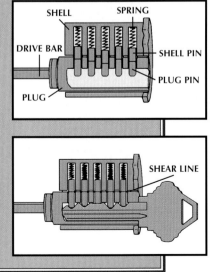

A key-in-knob lock.

The knob on the outside of this model is keyed, while the inner knob has a thumb turn or button that can immobilize the outer one. Either knob works the lock, since each is linked through a stem to a retractor that connects to the beveled latch and plunger. As the door—locked or unlocked—swings shut, the lip of the strike plate pushes back both pieces. A ridge in the plunger arm raises the retainer bar *(inset, top),* permitting a notch in the latch arm to slide past and the arm to retract fully. When the door is completely shut, the latch springs out again into the strike box, but the retainer bar pins the plunger in place.

If the inside button is set in the locking position, the latch cannot be forced back because the retainer bar, no longer supported by the ridge on the retracted plunger, catches in the notch in the latch arm. Turning a key or the inside knob moves an unlocking arm *(inset, bottom)* that raises the retainer bar and permits the latch to be withdrawn.

The outside knob cannot withdraw the locked latch because a pin attached to the locking button engages a notch in the stem of the outside knob, immobilizing that knob. If the inside button is set to the unlocked position, the pin is disengaged from the outside-knob stem; then either the inside or the outside knob can be turned to withdraw the latch, allowing the door to open.

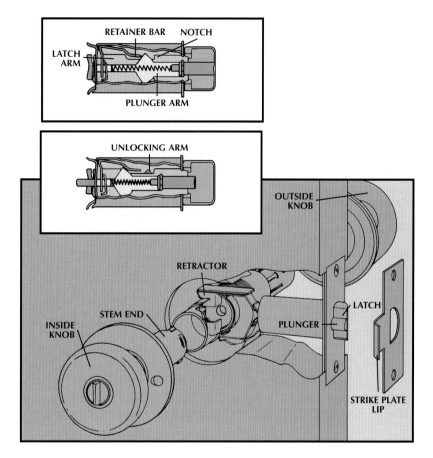

A rim lock.

The case of this lock, mounted on the inside of the door, aligns with a strike plate attached to the door-frame. A key from outside and a thumb turn inside operate the lock by turning a drive bar fitted to a catch that raises or lowers a plate encasing the two vertical bolts, which slide into rings in the strike.

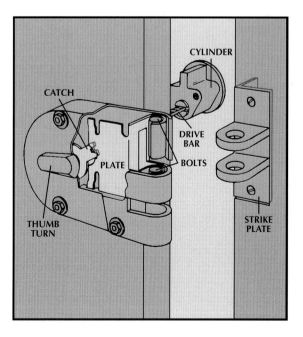

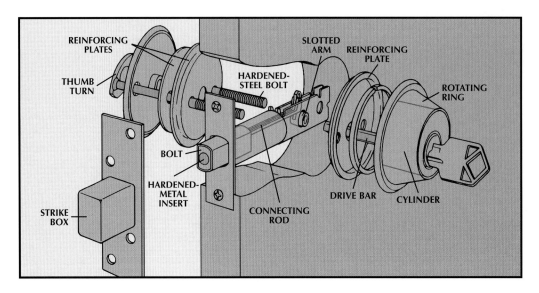

A deadbolt lock.

A key from the outside and either a key or a thumb turn from the inside rotate a drive bar that fits into a slotted arm in the bolt assembly. The arm pulls or pushes a connecting rod to move the bolt into or out of the strike box. In a good deadbolt lock, the bolt projects 1 inch or more from the door edge and is made of hardened metal or has hardened-metal inserts to resist sawing. Hardened-steel bolts secure the cylinder. Reinforcing plates and rings prevent the cylinder and bolts from being pulled out of the door. A beveled rotating ring, difficult to grip or crush, circles the face of the cylinder. And in models intended for wood doors an internal shield keeps the deadbolt from being forced back with a sharp tool such as an ice pick.

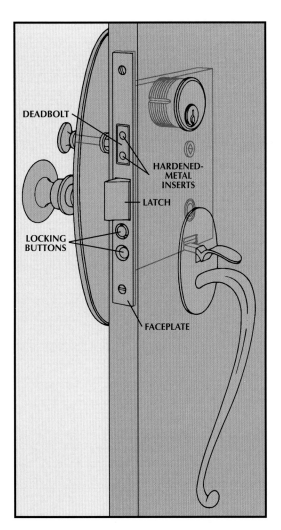

A mortise lock.

This versatile lock combines a spring latch and a deadbolt in a single unit that fits into a large cutout, or mortise, in the edge of the door. The bolt is locked with a key. A button in the faceplate on the edge of the door immobilizes the thumbpiece, which operates the latch. A second button frees the thumbpiece.

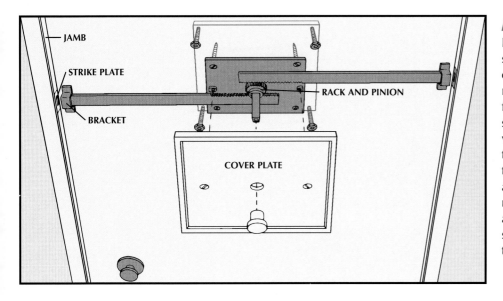

JAMB

STRIKE PLATE

BRACKET

RACK AND PINION

COVER PLATE

A double-bar lock.

In this high-security lock, designed mainly for doors that open outward, long steel bars run horizontally along the inside face of the door and slide into strike plates anchored to the vertical studs on each side of the door. The bolts are secured to the door with brackets and are moved by a rack-and-pinion mechanism that is operated by an exterior keylock and an inside thumb turn set in the center of the door.

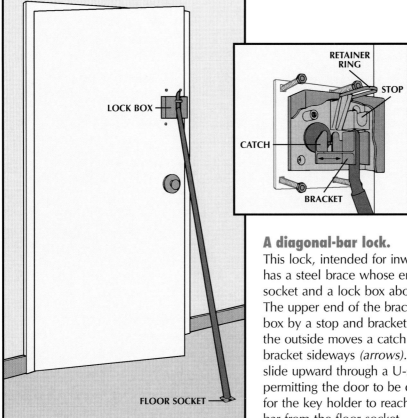

LOCK BOX

RETAINER RING

STOP

CATCH

BRACKET

FLOOR SOCKET

A diagonal-bar lock.

This lock, intended for inward-opening doors, has a steel brace whose ends fit in a floor socket and a lock box above the doorknob. The upper end of the brace is secured in the box by a stop and bracket *(inset)*. A key from the outside moves a catch that pushes the bracket sideways *(arrows)*. The bar can then slide upward through a U-shaped retainer ring, permitting the door to be opened far enough for the key holder to reach inside and lift the bar from the floor socket.

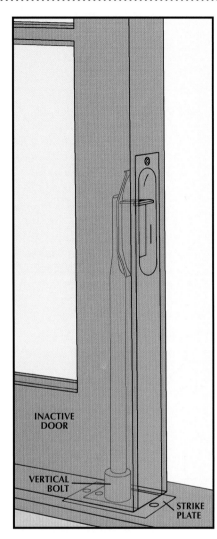

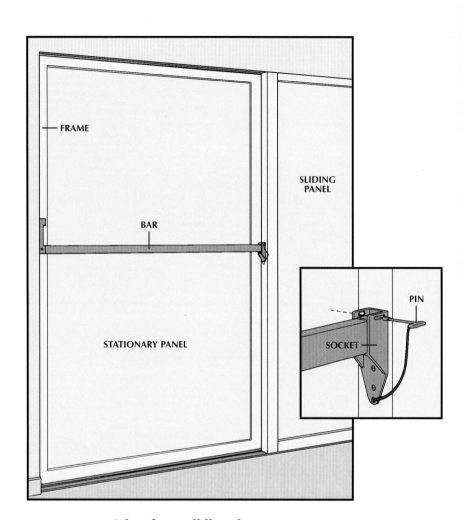

Bolts for a French door.

Recessed in the top and bottom edges of one-half of a pair of French doors—whichever door is opened less frequently—vertical bolts lock into strikes in the threshold *(above)* and top jamb. The bolts cannot be dislodged by force or unlocked by hand through a broken pane of glass. The other door is fitted with a double-cylinder deadbolt lock.

A bar for a sliding door.

A pivoted metal bar drops from the doorframe to a socket on the edge of the sliding panel to lock this door securely in place. A pin across the socket *(inset)* holds the bar in position and is pulled out to open the lock. When not needed, the bar swings up into a bracket on the doorframe.

Adding a deadbolt.

For extra security, a keyed deadbolt mounted at either the head or the base of the doors *(right)* locks the movable and stationary panels together, so that the sliding panel cannot be pushed open or lifted from its frame. (See page 31 for another way to block lifting of the movable panel.)

Padlocks and hasps.

A good padlock has a hardened-steel shackle, a lock case of solid brass or laminated steel, and a five-pin cylinder. A key turn rotates the cylinder and a rectangular drive bar, retracting the bolts from notches in the shackle *(inset)*. The shackle then pops up, propelled by a spring near the lock base. In locking, a downward thrust on the shackle forces the beveled bolts back until the shackle notches can engage them.

The ring of the hasp, called a staple, should be hardened steel. The hasp edges should be beveled to ward off prying attacks.

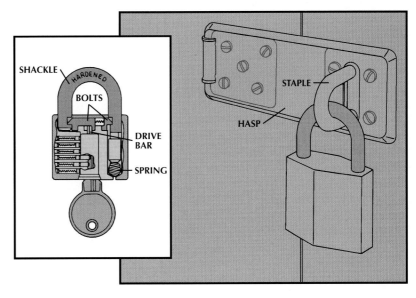

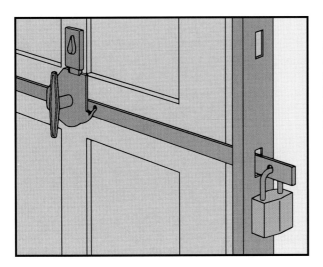

A second lock for a garage door.

A padlock in a hole drilled through the end of a garage door bolt secures the bolt even if the door's regular lock mechanism is destroyed. Many garage door bolts come with a predrilled hole.

TRICKS OF THE TRADE

Stopping a Garage Door in Its Tracks

Some garage doors have bolts that are long enough to pass through the track but too short to be padlocked as shown above. To double the security of such a door, loop the shackle of a padlock through one of the holes in the track, positioning the lock immediately above one of the rollers when the door is shut.

Improving the utility or security of a lock may be as simple as changing the key, but frequently a new lock is the answer. A rim lock, a deadbolt lock, or vertical bolts for a French door *(page 46)* can be added without your having to change the hardware that is already there. If you are replacing a key-in-knob lock, purchase a model that fits in the existing holes; otherwise you may need a new door. A mortise lock always requires a new door.

Rekeying: If you lose a key, have the cylinder of the lock rekeyed by a locksmith. Make sure that the cylinder is of the tamper-resistant type described on page 32; otherwise, replace it.

Rekeying or replacing a cylinder necessitates disassembly of the lock. In deadbolt locks *(page 34)*, you can free the cylinder entirely. In many key-in-knob locks, however, you will have to stop once you free the outside knob. Take the knob, with the cylinder still inside, to a locksmith, along with an old key.

Matching Lock and Door: Before buying a new lock set, make sure the door is thick enough for the bolt mechanism. In a panel door, the vertical stile on the edge of the door must be wide enough for knobs and their decorative roses. With a mortise lock, the stile must be sufficiently wide so that the mortise does not weaken the joint between the stile and the connecting horizontal rail.

If you plan to purchase a lock with a beveled latch (found on key-in-knob locks, mortise locks, and some rim locks), you will need to specify the so-called hand of the door. To determine this, first note which way the door swings. If, like most exterior doors, it opens inward, stand outside and look at the hinge position. Hinges on the right identify a right-hand door, hinges on the left a left-hand door. If the door opens outward, it takes a lock that is normally installed on a door of the opposite hand.

Improving the Lock Strength: Check the screws that come with the lock and replace any that are too short to provide good security *(page 27)*. When installing a rim lock, replace the mounting screws for its case with carriage bolts and nuts *(page 44)*.

TOOLS

Screwdrivers
Open-end
  wrenches
Groove-joint pliers
Hammer
Hole saw
Electric drill with
  twist bits and
  spade bits
Utility knife
Wood chisels

MATERIALS

Electrician's tape
Lipstick or grease pencil

SECURITY WITH OR WITHOUT A KEY

Fumbling for a key slot in the dark or trying to fish keys from purse or pocket with an armful of groceries can be a nuisance; to forget or lose a key and be locked out of the house is more exasperating still. One way to avoid such problems is to install a combination lock like the one shown at right, in which the knob serves as the dial. In addition to a regular three- or four-digit combination, set by the homeowner, the locks can be given a second combination that allows maintenance workers or other nonresidents access to the house at times controlled by the homeowner.

These locks also function with a normal key, for those who want quick access without having to dial a combination.

REPLACING CYLINDERS

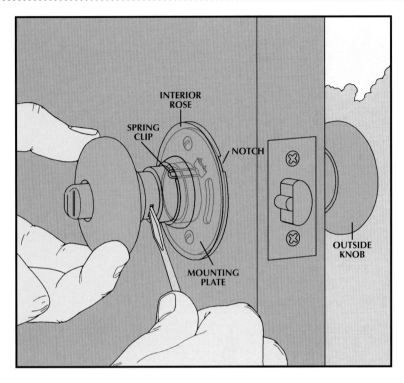

Key-in-knob lock.
If screws secure the interior rose, remove them. If none are visible, use the tip of a screwdriver to depress the small metal tab projecting through a slot behind the knob. Pull the knob from the lock set, push in the spring clip that protrudes from the rose, and insert a screwdriver into the notch at the rim of the rose to pry the rose away. Remove the two screws in the mounting plate under the rose, and from the exterior side of the door, pull the outside knob, which contains the lock cylinder.

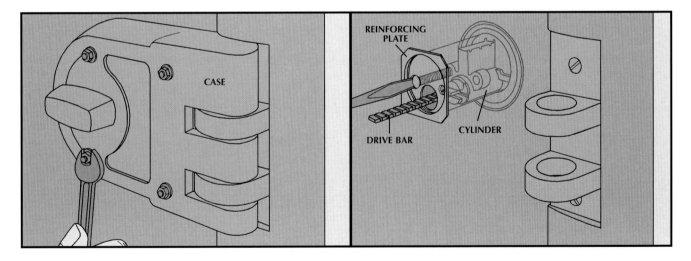

Rim lock.
With the door unlocked, remove the screws or nuts that secure the lock case *(above, left)*. Wiggle the case off the door and the cylinder drive bar, then remove the screws of the reinforcing plate *(above, right)*, and from outside the door, pull out the cylinder.

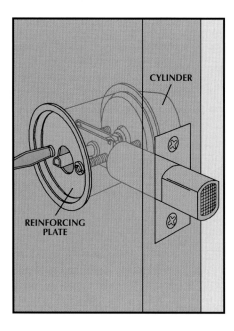

Deadbolt lock.

Remove the rose to expose the reinforcing plate; remove the screws holding the plate to free the cylinder. If the lock has no reinforcing plate, removing the interior rose frees the cylinder.

On a double-cylinder lock with both interior and exterior cylinders, loosen the screws that extend through the inside cylinder to free both cylinders. If these screws are nonreversible or if they have been damaged so they cannot be removed *(page 47)*, have a locksmith remove the cylinder.

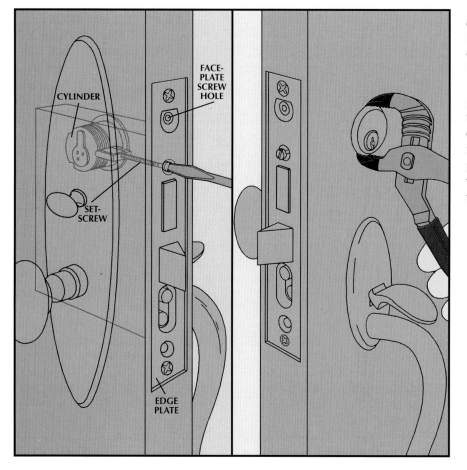

Mortise lock.

Find the small setscrew located on the edge plate of the door at the same height as the lock cylinder. (Sometimes it is hidden behind a decorative faceplate.) Back the setscrew out three or four turns *(far left)*. From outside the door, unscrew the cylinder. If it does not turn easily, grip it with groove-joint pliers whose jaws have been covered with electrician's tape to prevent them from marring the cylinder *(near left)*.

ADDING A DEADBOLT

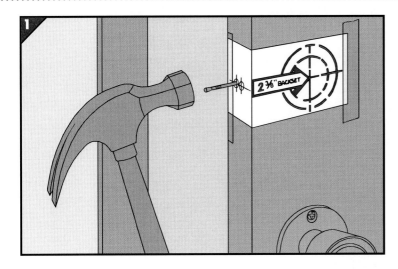

1. Marking the holes.
◆ Tape the paper template that came with the lock to the edge and face of the door about 6 inches above the knob.
◆ Mark each screw hole by driving a finishing nail $\frac{1}{4}$ inch through the marks on the paper template, making sure the nail remains perpendicular to the surface. To allow for variations in door thickness, some templates are marked with alternate locations for drilling the edge holes; be sure to use the mark specified for the size of your door.

2. Boring the cylinder hole.
With the door closed, or firmly wedged open, use a hole saw to bore a cylinder hole the size that is specified by the manufacturer. To avoid splintering the thin veneer of the door face as the teeth of the saw exit, stop drilling as soon as the small center bit of the saw breaks through the opposite side and complete the hole from that side of the door.

3. Drilling the bolt hole.
Wedge the door open. To make sure that the bit stays on course as you drill into the narrow edge of the door, enlist a helper. While you watch from above to keep the bit from straying right or left, have the helper check that it remains horizontal.

Alternatively, use a drill guide (box, page 42) to ensure that holes are drilled perfectly.

Taking the Guesswork Out of Drilling

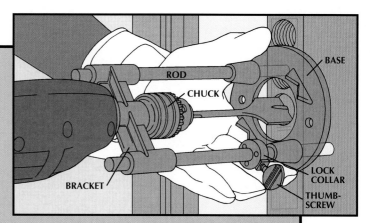

A drill guide offers a sure way of drilling a hole straight and perpendicular. The model seen here consists of a bracket to hold the drill, a pair of runners that slide along two metal rods, a lock collar to stop the drill when the bit has reached a predetermined depth, and a round base. The rod ends are set flush with the base when the drill guide is used on a door face. They are pushed partway through the base when the guide is used to steady a drill bit on a door edge, as shown here.

Before using the guide on a door edge, wrap the protruding rods in masking tape to avoid marring the door. Then, holding the base against a door edge with one hand, rotate the base clockwise to press the rods firmly against the door faces *(right)*. The drill's torque will help hold the guide rods in position as the hole is drilled.

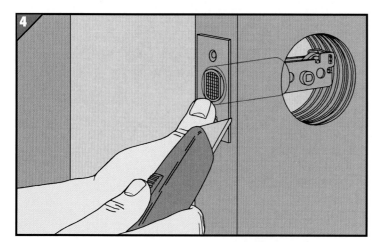

4. Seating the bolt assembly.
◆ Insert the bolt assembly into the bolt hole, then scribe the outline of the faceplate with a utility knife. The line left by a sharp knife is thinner and more precise than a pencil line.
◆ Chisel a mortise in the marked area for the faceplate, carving only as deep as the plate is thick.
◆ Fasten the assembly with screws.

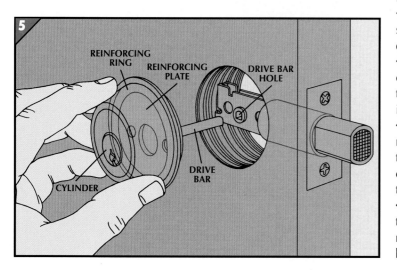

5. Installing the lock.
◆ For a deadbolt with thumb turn *(left)*, assemble the cylinder, drive bar, and the reinforcing plate and ring as directed by the manufacturer.
◆ Fit the assembly into the cylinder hole from outside the door, inserting the drive bar through the drive bar hole in the bolt assembly.
◆ Screw the rear reinforcing plate, if any, to the cylinder hole from inside the door, then set the thumb turn against the door, fitting the drive bar into the hole in the thumb turn.
◆ Insert mounting bolts through the thumb turn, the reinforcing plate, and the bolt assembly and screw them into the back of the cylinder. For a double-cylinder lock, fit the drive bars of both cylinders into the drive bar hole.
◆ Test the deadbolt with both the key and the thumb turn. If the bolt will not move in or out, remove the drive bar from the cylinder, rotate the bar 180 degrees, and reassemble the lock.

6. Marking for the strike box.

◆ Coat the end of the bolt with lipstick or a grease pencil, close the door, and turn the bolt against the jamb, leaving a mark on it.

◆ At the mark, bore a hole for the strike box in the jamb, drilling with the same bit used for the bolt hole in the door. If you hit a finishing nail, chisel around it until you can pull it out with pliers.

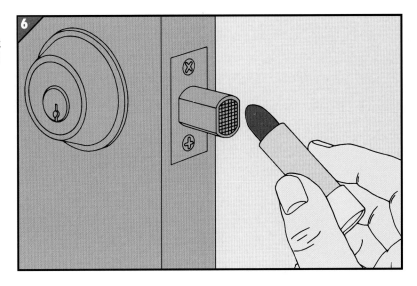

INSTALLING A SPRING LATCH

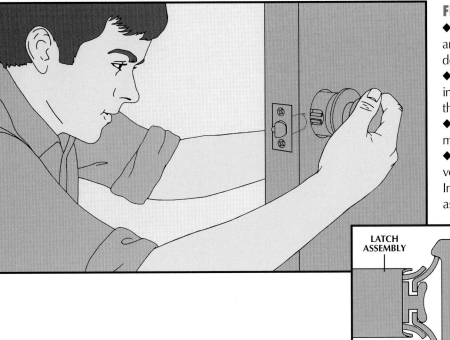

Fitting the lock.

◆ Drill a cylinder hole and a bolt hole and mortise the latch assembly as for a deadbolt lock *(pages 41-42, Steps 1-4)*.

◆ From the outside, set the lock body in place, engaging the end pieces of the latch assembly *(inset)*.

◆ From the inside, screw the inner mounting plate to the lock body.

◆ Install the interior rose and knob, reversing the steps described on page 39. Install the strike plate in the same way as for a deadbolt strike *(above)*.

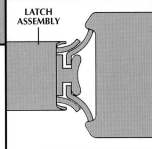

LATCH
ASSEMBLY

THE RIGHT WAY TO ATTACH A RIM LOCK

1. Mounting the lock.

◆ Bore a hole for the cylinder about 6 inches above the doorknob.

◆ Insert the cylinder from the outside, screw the rear reinforcing plate to it, and set the lock case against the door so that the drive bar fits into the thumb turn slot of the case. If necessary, shorten the drive bar by snapping it at one of the grooves with pliers.

◆ Bore holes for the attachment bolts, using the lock case to locate the holes.

◆ Bolt on the lock case, placing lock washers and nuts on the interior side of the door.

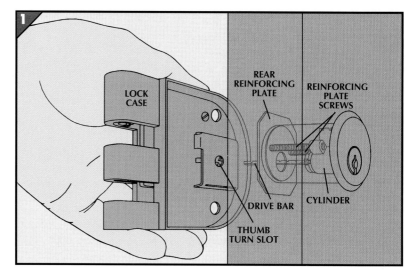

2. Mortising for the strike.

When you are chiseling the mortises for the strike, pare away small amounts of wood and periodically test the mortise depth until the lock bolts slip easily into the rings. If you cut too deeply, shim behind the strike with cardboard.

◆ With the door closed, score lines in those places where the top and bottom of the lock case meet

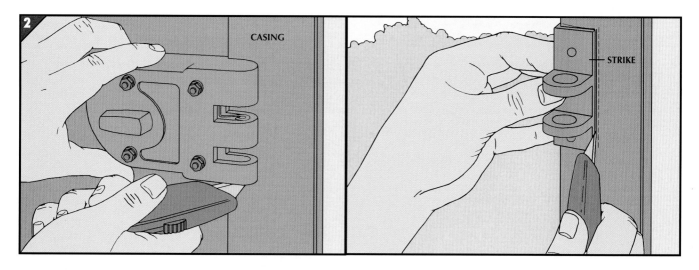

the door casing (above, left).

◆ With the door open, hold the strike between these marks and score a vertical line along the outer edge of the strike (above, right).

◆ To allow for the part of the strike that wraps around the jamb, mark a second vertical line farther out on the door casing by a distance equal to the thickness of the strike (dashed line).

◆ Tap a chisel, bevel side in, along the outermost marks to cut straight into the casing; then, holding the chisel bevel side down, pare out the wood within the marked area.

◆ Mark the jamb mortise by holding the strike in the casing mortise. Score around it, and chisel out a recess in the jamb as you did in the casing.

A MORTISE LOCK

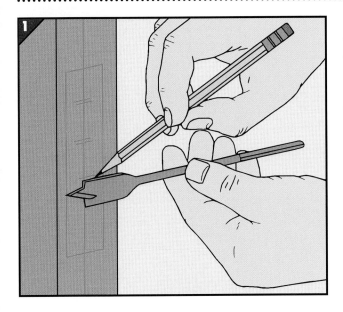

1. Starting the mortise.
This lock fits inside a deep mortise in the thin edge of the door and requires precision work best done with a special drill guide *(box, page 42)*; a bit wandering even slightly can ruin an expensive door.
◆ Use the manufacturer's template to locate the knob and cylinder holes, then outline the mortise on the door edge.
◆ Use a spade bit as wide as the mortise to make a series of marks down the mortise to indicate drilling locations, spacing the top and bottom marks for adjoining holes about $\frac{1}{4}$ inch apart *(left)*.
◆ Use the bit and drill guide, set to the depth of the mortise, to drill the holes.

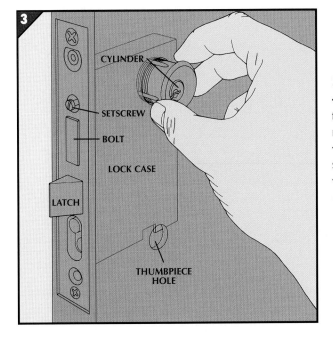

2. Chiseling the mortise.
◆ Chip the remaining wood out of the mortise with a chisel and mallet. Make many small cuts rather than a few large ones to keep the chisel from biting too deeply.
◆ Finish up the mortise by holding the chisel with the beveled side facing into the cavity and shaving the walls flat without a mallet.
◆ Drill holes for the thumbpieces, knob, and cylinder, taking care to drill all the way into the mortise.
◆ Set the lock into the mortise and, holding it straight up and down along the edge of the door, mark the shallow faceplate mortise *(page 42, Step 4)*.
◆ Chisel out the faceplate mortise and screw in the lock.

3. Installing the cylinder and trim.
◆ From outside, screw the threaded cylinder into the lock case and secure it with the setscrew, which runs from the edge plate into the lock.
◆ Attach the outside thumbpiece or knob, the inside thumb turn and knob, and the trim.
◆ Install the strike as you would for a deadbolt *(page 43, Step 6)*.

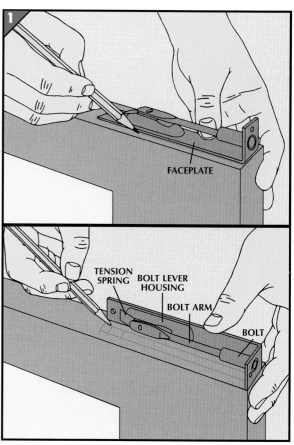

FACEPLATE

TENSION SPRING **BOLT LEVER HOUSING** **BOLT ARM** **BOLT**

VERTICAL BOLTS FOR FRENCH DOORS

1. Marking the mortise.

◆ Remove the inactive door—the door that is usually closed—from its hinges.

◆ Center the bolt assembly facedown on the edge of the door, flush with the top edge, and trace the outline of the faceplate to indicate the area of the main mortise *(right, top)*. Draw a centerline through this area, parallel to the door edge.

◆ Lay the bolt assembly on its side *(right, bottom),* and make marks at the end of the bolt arm tension spring, at the end of the bolt arm, and at the point where the bolt arm engages the bolt. In addition, mark the position of the bolt lever housing. The marks serve as guides for cutting the sloping lock assembly mortise.

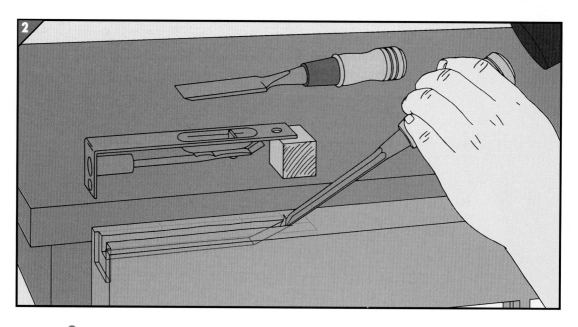

2. Cutting the mortise.

◆ Using the marks as guides, chisel the mortise to accommodate the tension spring, the bolt lever housing, the bolt arm, and the bolt. For each mortise section, use a chisel that is as wide as the corresponding part of the assembly, and cut each section only as deep as is necessary for fit.

◆ Mortise the door edge and top for the faceplate, then screw the assembly in place.

◆ Repeat Steps 1 and 2 at the bottom of the door, then rehang the door and install strike plates in the top jamb and in the threshold *(page 43, Step 6).*

Windows That Cannot Be Forced Open

Most windows pose little deterrent to intruders, since inserting a knife blade between the sashes is generally all it takes to throw a latch. And unless the panes are made of special plastic *(pages 50-51)*, burglars can cut or break the glass and reach inside. To guard against such attacks, install one of the locks shown here on all windows that are accessible from outside.

For safety's sake, lock any window that might become an emergency exit in a fire in such a way that it can be opened quickly from inside. For convenience, make sure one key will open all locked windows, and store the key where it is handy from inside but cannot be fished for from outside.

Double-Hung Windows: One way to secure the common double-hung

window—two wooden sashes that slide up and down in a frame—is to replace the standard thumb latch with a keyed unit. But two weaknesses make the keyed latch ineffective: First, like all locks anchored with common screws, it can be unscrewed. And even the remedy for this shortcoming—defacing the heads of the screws that come with the lock or fastening it with one-way screws *(below)*—will not keep an intruder from loosening the latch with a pry bar.

More resistant locks rely on a metal shaft that pierces both sashes and holds them tightly together *(page 48)*. Mounted near the side of the window rather than in the middle, such locks are relatively pry resistant, and they can secure

a window in two positions—closed or partly open for ventilation. A wedge-type lock *(page 49)*, another strong barrier against break-ins, shares this feature. It comes with strike plates for both the open and shut positions.

Sliding or Casement Windows: More difficult to lock than double-hung windows, horizontally sliding glass windows are best secured by the methods used for sliding doors *(page 36)*. Casement windows also present security challenges. If they open with a crank, either remove the crank handle from the shaft, putting it near the window but out of a burglar's sight and reach, or replace the standard latch with one that must be locked with a key *(page 49)*.

TOOLS

Electric drill with bits ($\frac{3}{16}$", $\frac{1}{4}$", and $\frac{5}{8}$")

Conical grindstone bit
Wire cutters
Awl
Screwdriver

MATERIALS

Common nails (3")
Nonretractable sheet-metal screws

SAFETY TIPS

Wear goggles to protect your eyes when drilling.

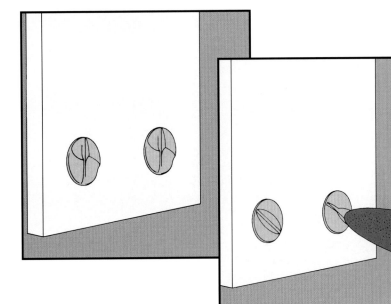

Putting in screws for keeps.
A special head on nonretractable screws *(far left)* makes them impossible to remove without destroying screw or framing. Before tightening such screws, be certain that the lock is positioned correctly.

If nonretractable screws are not readily available, erase the slot in the head of conventional screws using a conical grindstone in an electric drill *(near left)*. Grind only along the sides of the slot; excessive grinding can weaken the screw, making it vulnerable to prying.

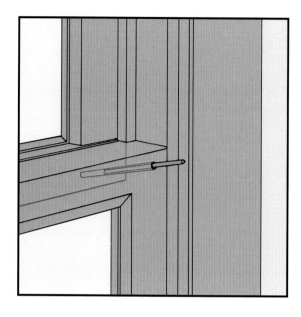

Locking a window with a nail.

◆ Drill a $\frac{3}{16}$-inch hole through the top rail of the bottom sash and at least $\frac{1}{2}$ inch into the bottom rail of the top sash. Angle the hole slightly downward so that the nail cannot fall out if the window is rattled.

◆ Trim the head from a 3-inch common nail with wire cutters so that the nail is just out of reach when slipped into the hole.

◆ Keep a magnet near the window to retrieve the nail and unlock the window.

Fitting a rod lock.

◆ Holding the body of the lock against the top rail of the bottom sash, locate a rod hole that misses the glass in both sashes. Mark holes for the rod and mounting screws with an awl.

◆ Drill holes for the mounting screws, then tape a $\frac{1}{4}$-inch bit for a hole about $2\frac{3}{8}$ inches deep and drill the hole for the rod.

◆ Screw the lock body to the sash.

◆ To allow ventilation, open the bottom sash no more than 4 inches, insert the rod in the lock to mark the top sash for a second rod hole, and drill a $\frac{1}{4}$-inch hole about $\frac{1}{2}$ inch deep.

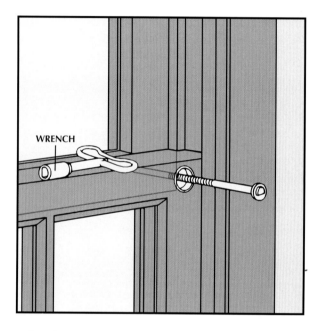

WRENCH

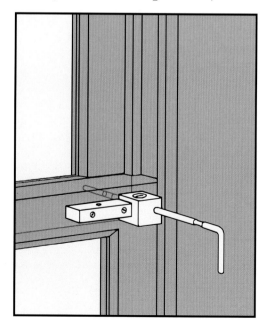

A lag bolt lock.

◆ Drill a $\frac{1}{4}$-inch hole through the top rail of the bottom sash and about halfway into the bottom rail of the top sash. Position the hole about $\frac{1}{2}$ inch from both the window frame and the top of the bottom sash to miss the glass.

◆ Enlarge the first $\frac{1}{4}$ inch of the hole with a $\frac{5}{8}$-inch bit for the metal shield at the head of the lag bolt.

◆ Slip the shield onto the bolt and screw it in place with the wrench provided by the manufacturer.

STILE

A wedge lock.
◆ When the window is closed, place the lock on top of the lower sash and mark the line where the top of the lock meets the stile of the top sash.
◆ Position the strike plate on the top sash so that its top barely covers the line, and mark the locking and mounting holes.
◆ Using a $\frac{5}{8}$-inch bit, drill $\frac{3}{8}$-inch holes for the locking posts; drill smaller holes for the mounting screws provided by the manufacturer.
◆ Mount the second strike plate 4 inches above the first to allow for ventilation.

A KEYED LATCH IN A CASEMENT WINDOW

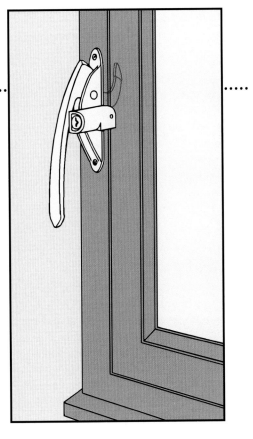

Installing a locking latch.
◆ Open the old latch and unscrew it from the window frame.
◆ Fit a keyed latch into the slot in the frame and fasten it with nonretractable sheet-metal screws.

Locking latches are made to fit most metal casement windows; when purchasing the latch, however, specify whether it is to fit on the left or the right side of the window.

Plastic windowpanes, far superior to glass in protecting against break-in, offer two levels of security. Acrylic plastic (often known by one of its trade names, Plexiglas) generally stops a thrown rock but breaks if attacked with a hammer. It is often used in garages and outbuildings, where vandalism is more of a concern than burglary is.

Polycarbonate resin plastic (which goes by the trade names Lexan and Hyzod) is even stronger—it can withstand a sledgehammer blow—but it is about twice as expensive as acrylic.

Preparing the Frame: If the glass is held in place by glazing compound—found on wood frames and some metal frames—brush linseed oil on the compound, wait 30 minutes for the oil to soften it, then scrape it off with a chisel. If linseed oil doesn't work, warm the compound with a heat gun set to a low temperature and held 10 to 15 inches away.

Beneath the glazing compound, glazier's points secure the pane in a wood frame; spring clips serve that purpose on some metal frames. Spring clips can be removed by hand to free the glass (opposite). Force glazier's points away from the pane with a putty knife, pull them out with long-nose pliers, and push the pane out of the sash. Clean the channel with a wire brush, then sand and paint it—silicone-base caulk bonds better to paint than to bare wood.

Working with Plastics: To determine the size of the new pane, measure the length and width of the sash between the bottoms of the glass channels. To allow for expansion (unless you are working in weather hotter than 85°F) subtract $\frac{1}{16}$ inch from each dimension.

Plastic sheets closely correspond to the standard thicknesses of window glass. For extra security, consider sheets that are $\frac{3}{16}$ or $\frac{1}{4}$ inch thick for a wood sash if the channel is wide enough to accommodate them. In the case of a metal sash, the new plastic pane must match the old glass in thickness.

Install plastic panes as shown on the facing page. For ordinary glazing compound, which cracks when subjected to the thermal expansion and contraction of sheet plastic, substitute a silicone-base window-and-door caulk. And because both types of plastic scratch more readily than glass, leave the protective shipping paper on until the work is finished.

 TOOLS

Chisel
Heat gun
Long-nose pliers
Circular saw or
 saber saw

Framing square
Wire brush
Paintbrush
Caulking gun
Putty knife
Clamps

 **MATERIALS**

Linseed oil
Naphtha
Paint

Silicone-base
 window-and-
 door caulk
Glazier's points

 **SAFETY TIPS**

Wear gloves when removing glass panes from a sash. Goggles protect your eyes when you are sawing plastic sheeting.

CHOOSING A SAW BLADE

	Thickness	Circular Saw Teeth per inch	Saber Saw Teeth per inch
Acrylic	$\frac{1}{16}" - \frac{1}{10}"$	6–8	18
	$\frac{1}{10}" - \frac{1}{3}"$	5–6	10–14
	more than $\frac{1}{3}"$	3–4	6
Polycarbonate Resin	$\frac{1}{16}" - \frac{1}{10}"$	10–12	10–18
	more than $\frac{1}{10}"$	3–5	8–12

Cutting plastic.
Plastic sheets can be cut with a circular saw or saber saw. The type of blade depends on the material and its thickness. With circular saws, best results are obtained using a plywood finishing blade adjusted to protrude no more than $\frac{1}{16}$ inch through the material to avoid chipping. In saber saws, use a metal-cutting blade.

SETTING PLASTIC IN A WOOD SASH

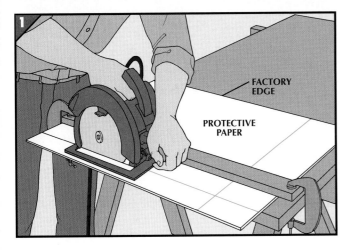

FACTORY EDGE

PROTECTIVE PAPER

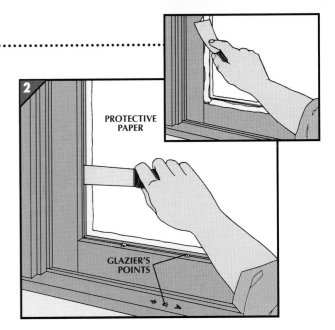

PROTECTIVE PAPER

GLAZIER'S POINTS

1. Cutting the pane to size.
◆ Mark the windowpane dimensions on two adjacent factory edges of the plastic sheet, then draw the other two edges on the protective paper with a pencil and a framing square.
◆ Clamp a straight board parallel to the marked line to guide the saw, and cut slowly along the line. Pushing the saw too fast will chip the plastic.
◆ Peel back 1 inch of the protective paper from each edge of the new pane and cut away the paper with scissors, taking care not to scratch the plastic.
◆ Wash the exposed plastic with mild detergent and water. If any adhesive remains, wipe it away with naphtha.

2. Installing the pane.
◆ Clean and paint the sash channels.
◆ When the paint dries, apply a $\frac{1}{4}$-inch bead of silicone-base caulk in the channels, center the pane in the opening, and press it into the caulk.
◆ Using a putty knife, press glazier's points into the window frame at 4-inch intervals to hold the pane in place.
◆ Apply a bead of caulk around the edges of the pane, covering the glazier's points. Smooth the bead to a bevel (inset).
◆ When the caulk has cured, peel the paper from both sides of the pane, dissolve any adhesive that remains with naphtha, and wash the plastic with mild detergent.

PROCEDURES FOR METAL SASHES

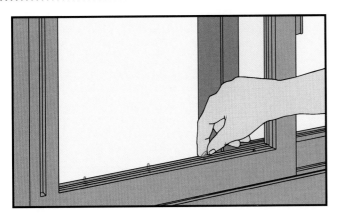

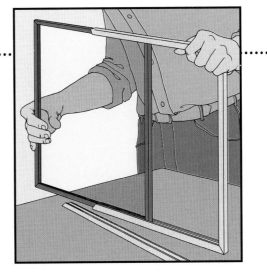

A sash with metal clips.
◆ If the channels are sealed with glazing compound, remove it. Then pinch together the now-exposed spring clips, and pull them out of their holes. Push the old pane out of the sash.
◆ Line the channel with silicone-base caulk, press the plastic pane into the caulk, and replace the clips.
◆ Cover the clips with caulk and bevel it neatly.

A sash with rubber gaskets.
◆ If the glass is held by U-shaped rubber gaskets, unscrew one side of the sash and pull it off, then slide gaskets and glass out.
◆ Fit the gaskets onto the new pane, slide it into the sash, and refasten the side piece you removed.

A ready-made, adjustable steel grille is an easy-to-install barrier for a window. For maximum protection, it should be mounted inside, but because this prevents easy operation of the window sash, the usual position is outside. Grilles of this type are fastened to the sides of the window frame.

Attaching a Grille to Wood: In many modern frame homes the outside window recess is so shallow that the only attachment available is the brickmold. Generally this exterior wood trim is only $\frac{3}{4}$ inch thick, insufficient for long screws; as a result, the grille may not foil a determined burglar, although it can deter an intruder. In older homes, where the window is recessed more than 2 inches from the outer face of the wall, grilles can be screwed through the jamb into a stud.

Attaching to Masonry: If the window frame is masonry, use expansion anchors *(opposite)*. The holding power of the anchors depends on the composition of the wall—concrete is strongest, brick weakest—and on the tightness of pilot holes. In old, powdery masonry, the bit size recommended by the anchor manufacturer may make too large a hole; experiment with smaller bits.

With brick walls, locate the anchors in horizontal mortar joints, not the weaker vertical joints or the middle of a brick. The outside diameter of the anchor should match the thickness of the joints (usually $\frac{3}{8}$ inch).

A Final Precaution: To prevent a burglar from removing the grille fasteners, use screws with one-way heads. If you cannot obtain them or must make do with larger fasteners—lag screws, machine bolts, or machine nuts—erase the screw slot or round the bolt or nut with a grinder *(page 47)*.

TOOLS

Hammer drill with carbide bit (solid concrete wall)
Electric drill with masonry bit (brick wall)
Electric drill with twist bits (high-speed steel for metal, carbon steel for wood)
Hammer
Center punch

MATERIALS

Window grille
Masonry anchors
Wood screws ($1\frac{1}{4}$" No. 12)
Lag screws ($\frac{1}{4}$" x $2\frac{1}{2}$") and washers

SAFETY TIPS

Wear safety goggles to protect your eyes when hammering and drilling.

BRICKMOLD

Mounting an adjustable grille in wood.
Fasten a grille to the brickmold only if there is no other choice.

◆ Telescope the grille against the brickmold, center it vertically, and have a helper mark the inner edges of the brickmold through the holes in the mounting strips *(left)*.

◆ Drill pilot holes at the marks *(page 27, Step 1)* and fasten the grille with $1\frac{1}{4}$-inch-long No. 12 wood screws.

If you can fasten the grille through the window jamb into the studs, place it against the strip of wood (called a blind stop) next to the window sash, and attach it with $2\frac{1}{2}$-inch-long $\frac{1}{4}$-inch lag screws and washers.

Mounting an adjustable grille in masonry.

◆ Center the grille in the opening and mark each mounting strip at intervals of about 8 inches, setting the marks at horizontal mortar joints in a brick wall or at the centers of blocks in a masonry-block wall.
◆ Remove the grille and strike the strip with a center punch opposite each mark *(right).*
◆ Choose anchors appropriate to the wall *(below)* and drill holes in the strip for the fasteners.
◆ Replace the grille, mark each hole's location on the masonry, and drill holes for the anchors.
◆ Insert the anchors and fasten the grille to them. Stop tightening each fastener as soon as you feel substantial resistance.

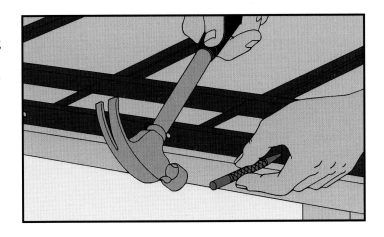

ANCHORS FOR MASONRY WALLS

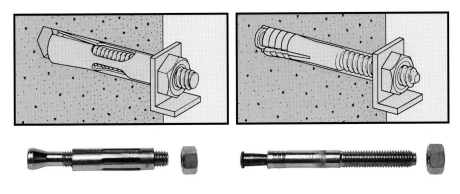

Threaded stud anchors.

Designed for use with a machine nut and a washer, these anchors get their strength from especially deep pilot holes. The anchor at far left tightens against the masonry when the nut forces a split sleeve over the bolt's mushroom-shaped end. The anchor at near left is tightened against the masonry by a few hammer blows that force the tapered pin into the split section of the shank; once tightened, the anchor cannot be removed.

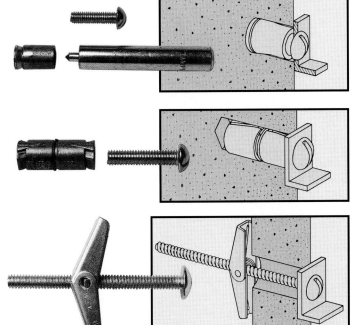

A hammer-set anchor.

Especially suitable for shallow holes, this anchor is set with a hammer and a special tool provided by the manufacturer. As the tool drives the lead sleeve down over the plug, the bottom of the plug forces the sleeve out against the masonry.

A drop-in anchor.

This anchor, suited to old or weak brick walls, is simply inserted into a snug pilot hole. As a machine screw or machine bolt is tightened, wedges at the ends of the anchor force the two sleeves apart, creating an even pressure along the entire length of the hole.

An anchor for concrete blocks.

This toggle bolt provides excellent holding power in weak materials such as crumbly cinder block. The toggle unfolds in the space inside a block and is pulled back against the wall of the block as the bolt is tightened.

Safes and Vaults for the House

For precious possessions and vitally important documents, the optimal safeguard against burglary and fire is a bank safe-deposit box. But most safe-deposit boxes are too small for bulky objects and too inconvenient for frequently used items—financial records, computer disks, and the like. The best way to protect such articles is to store them in a safe or in a strongroom that is burglary and fire resistant *(page 59)*.

Before choosing a safe, decide whether you are concerned more about burglary or fire, since few safes protect against both. Burglary safes have thick steel bodies, combination locks, and hardened-steel bolts, but papers inside may char in a fire. A fire safe has a double shell of thin sheet metal filled with insulation. Some have reinforced doors and combination locks, but thieves can crack them by peeling away the sheet metal.

Fire Safes: The insulation in a fire safe—lightweight concrete and vermiculite, a form of mica—contains as much as 30 quarts of water, which is released as steam in a fire, absorbing heat in the process. The

vapor filters through vents inside and outside the safe and may crumple and discolor papers, but they will remain legible and flexible enough to handle.

Look for the Underwriters Laboratories (UL) label on any fire safe you consider buying. It will indicate how long the unit can withstand a fire and how high the interior temperature may go. The label also specifies the safe's type: An "insulated filing device" shields papers from 1,700°F heat but may be torn open by falling debris; a "fire-resistant safe" and an "insulated record container" not only resist heat but protect against the effects of a collapsing building.

Burglary Safes: The most secure burglary safes are UL-rated models, which weigh 800 pounds or more; they are primarily designed for business use. Safes designed for the home tend to be lighter and less expensive, but they are also more vulnerable, able to withstand sledgehammers, drills, and pry bars for only a few minutes. If you buy a safe without an overall UL rating, evaluate it part by part. Look for a combi-

nation lock with a UL label; a UL-listed relocking device, which will fasten the bolts automatically if a burglar tries to drill through the lock or punch it out of its housing; a concealed hardened-steel plate to protect the lock and bolts; and bolts or steel hooks that secure the hinge side of the door.

Installing the Safe: Most people choose a freestanding safe of moderate size. To prevent a burglar from carting it away, fasten it to a floor or build it into a false wall *(pages 56-57)*; many dealers will arc weld angle irons or mounting brackets to the safe according to your specifications. Another option, if the safe is to stand on a concrete floor, is to increase its weight and strength either by having the supplier encase it in concrete or by building a shell of concrete blocks around it *(page 58)*.

Choose an inconspicuous or concealed location for the safe—beneath a stairway or behind a false electrical panel, for example. Protect the area with a photoelectric, infrared, or microwave sensor *(pages 77-78)*, discreetly placed so that it does not betray the safe's presence.

 TOOLS

Keyhole saw
Hammer
Electronic stud finder
Circular saw
Electric drill with bits ($\frac{1}{2}$", $\frac{1}{4}$", and conical grindstone)
Mortise chisel
Trowel
Cold chisel

 **MATERIALS**

2 x 4s
Common nails (2" and 3")
1 x 4 lumber
Angle irons ($\frac{1}{4}$" x $1\frac{1}{2}$" and $\frac{1}{4}$" x 3")
Carriage bolts ($\frac{1}{2}$" and 3")
Sheet-metal screws
Shims

Lag screws ($\frac{1}{2}$" x 2") and washers
Steel plates
Mortar
Wire mesh (6" x 6")
Bond-beam blocks
Reinforcing bars ($\frac{3}{8}$")
Tie wire
Concrete bricks or half-blocks

Plywood ($\frac{1}{2}$")
Type X wallboard ($\frac{5}{8}$")
Wallboard ($\frac{5}{8}$")
Solid-core door ($1\frac{3}{4}$")
Steel rods
Hinges ($4\frac{1}{2}$")
Deadbolt lock and maximum-security strike
Ventilators (6" x 8")

SAFETY TIPS *Goggles protect your eyes when you are hammering, chiseling, and using electric drills and power saws.*

Earplugs shield your ears from the noise of power tools operated in an enclosed space.

REPOSITORIES FOR YOUR VALUABLES

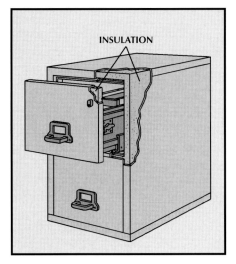

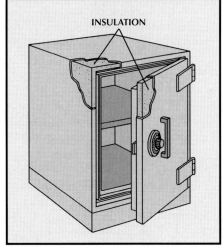

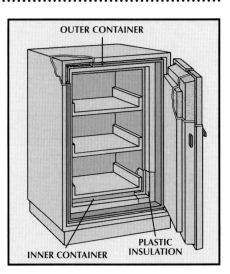

A fire-resistant file.
Sheet-metal shells sandwich 2-inch layers of fire-resistant insulation in this cabinet, which is available in one-, two-, and four-drawer sizes and can hold big objects or large amounts of paper. Additional insulation in the front panel of each drawer and in the horizontal partitions between drawers makes each drawer an independent compartment.

A safe for papers.
The safe above is called a Class 350 record safe because temperatures inside it will not exceed 350°F during a fire. In addition to its fire-resistant features, it is reinforced to protect against falling debris, and it possesses a UL-approved combination lock. The safe comes in models that can be mounted in a wall, fastened to the floor, or fitted with casters.

A safe for films and stamps.
This expensive low-temperature safe—a Class 150 record container—protects articles that are easily damaged by heat and high humidity. The outer container is built like an ordinary fire safe, but an airtight inner container of wood and insulating plastic shields the contents from the steam generated by the outer insulation.

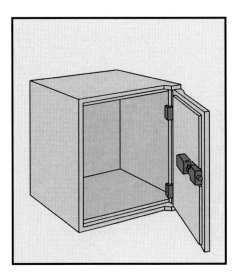

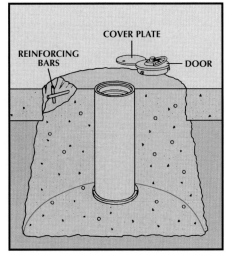

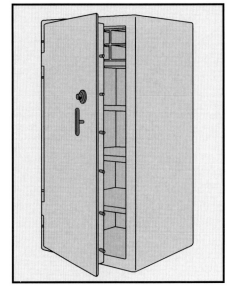

A burglary-resistant wall safe.
This 200-pound safe is made of $\frac{1}{2}$-inch steel, with seamless electric welds at all joints. Its door, a steel plate 1 inch thick, is fastened with a three-tumbler combination lock and a hardened-steel bolt. Heavy steel hooks interlock with a flange on the body to prevent an attack on the hinges.

A safe to bury in the floor.
Though awkwardly shaped and small, the safe above is inexpensive, easy to conceal, fire resistant, and difficult to crack. Almost all its strength is built into the $1\frac{3}{4}$-inch steel door, secured by three 1-inch bolts of hardened steel. A solid block of concrete reinforced with steel bars protects the body.

A security cabinet.
Meant for objects too large to fit inside an ordinary safe, this cabinet is 80 inches high, 30 inches wide, and weighs 1,000 pounds. Its body is $\frac{1}{4}$-inch steel plate, and its $\frac{3}{8}$-inch steel door is fastened by 12 steel bolts, 6 on each side.

BUILDING A SAFE INTO A WALL

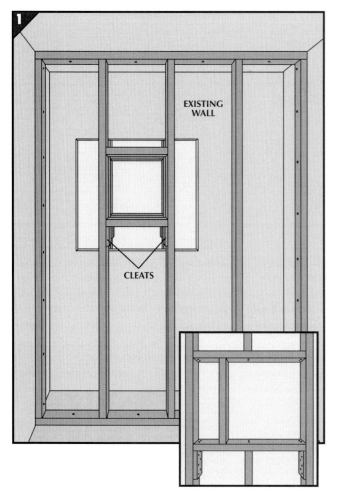

EXISTING WALL

CLEATS

1. Building a false wall.
For a burglary or fire safe that is narrower than the space between two wall studs, follow these steps:

◆ Cut away the wall covering around the planned location of the safe.

◆ Nail horizontal 2-by-4s between the studs of the existing wall, $\frac{1}{2}$ inch above and below the safe location; add 1-by-4 cleats under the lower 2-by-4. (If the safe is much narrower than the stud spacing, decrease the width of the frame by nailing a vertical 2-by-4 between the horizontal ones.)

◆ Cut a pair of 2-by-4s to serve as the top and bottom plates for the false wall.

◆ Use a stud finder to locate the ceiling joists and the unexposed wall studs. Mark the joists on the ceiling. Mark the plates with stud locations that match the existing studs.

◆ Nail the bottom plate to the floor, spacing it out from the existing wall to accommodate the depth of the safe.

◆ Nail studs to the top plate and slide this assembly over the bottom plate. Then nail the top plate to the ceiling joists and toenail the studs to the bottom plate.

◆ Make a cleated 2-by-4 frame in the new wall to match the one in the original wall.

For a safe wider than the stud spacing *(inset)*, cut away an existing stud 2 inches above and below the planned location of the new safe and build a frame as described above. Then nail the frame to the cut-off stud and add a vertical 2-by-4 to complete an opening the width of the safe.

2. Attaching the mounting brackets.
If you are installing a burglary safe that did not come with mounting flanges already attached, follow these steps:

◆ Drill $\frac{1}{2}$-inch holes at 4-inch intervals along the center of each flange of two $\frac{1}{4}$- by 1$\frac{1}{2}$-inch steel angle irons.

◆ Position one of the angle irons on one side of the safe, $\frac{1}{4}$ inch farther from the front than the thickness of the wallboard you are planning to hang, and use it as a template to drill matching holes through the sides of the safe *(right)*.

◆ Use the other angle as a template for drilling holes in the opposite side of the safe.

◆ Fasten the angles to the safe with $\frac{1}{2}$-inch carriage bolts, round boltheads facing out.

If you are installing a fire safe, attach brackets the same way, but drill $\frac{1}{4}$-inch holes in the angle flanges that fit against the safe. Then drill pilot holes into the shell of the safe—do not drill into the insulation—and secure the flanges with washers and self-tapping sheet-metal screws.

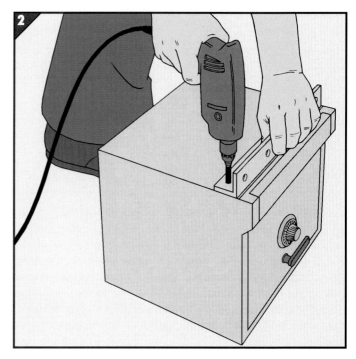

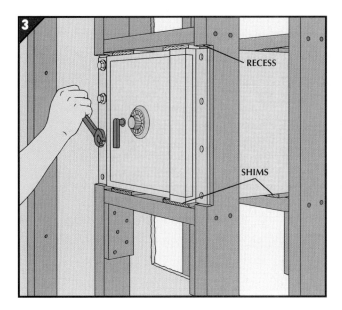

3. Installing the safe.

◆ Chisel a $\frac{1}{2}$-inch recess for the angle irons at the front of the mounting studs to make a flat surface for the wallboard.
◆ With a helper, slide the safe into the frame and shim the safe until it is level.
◆ Fasten the safe to the studs with $\frac{1}{2}$-inch lag screws 2 inches long and washers.
◆ Round the heads of the screws with a grinder to impede removal *(page 47)*.

BOLTING A SAFE TO THE FLOOR

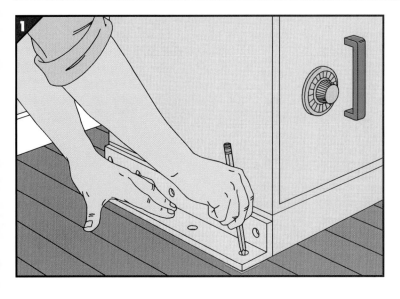

1. Marking the holes.

◆ Drill $\frac{1}{2}$-inch holes at 4-inch intervals along the center of each flange of two $\frac{1}{4}$- by 3-inch steel angle irons.
◆ Set the irons against the skirts at the sides of the safe as shown at left, and use the angles as templates to mark mounting holes on the skirts and the floor; in addition, mark the corners of the angles on the floor.
◆ Fasten the angles to the skirt with $\frac{1}{2}$-inch carriage bolts, the round boltheads facing out.

2. Fastening the safe.

◆ For a wood floor that is accessible from underneath, drill $\frac{1}{2}$-inch holes at the marks for 3-inch-long carriage bolts and attach the nuts from beneath, using drilled steel plates 3 inches square as washers.
◆ If you do not have access to the floor's underside, use $\frac{1}{2}$-inch lag screws and washers to fasten the safe to the subfloor or joists.

For a concrete floor, use one of the masonry fasteners shown on page 53. Drill pilot holes at least 3 inches deep, using a carbide-tipped masonry bit and a rented hammer drill, then fasten the safe with machine bolts.

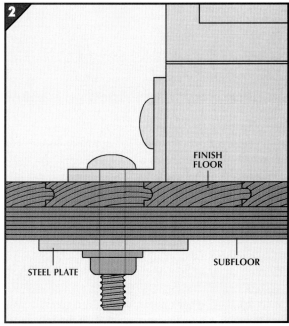

AN ENCLOSURE OF CONCRETE BLOCKS

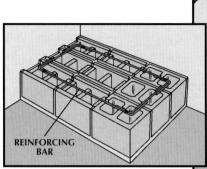

REINFORCING BAR

BOND-BEAM BLOCKS

CORNER BLOCKS

1. Building the base.

◆ At a corner of the basement floor lay a $\frac{3}{4}$-inch mortar bed at least 32 inches wider and 8 inches deeper than the safe.
◆ Cover the bed with 6- by 6-inch wire mesh and add another $\frac{3}{4}$ inch of mortar.
◆ Working from the corner, cover all of the mortar except the shorter of its two outer edges with a course of bond-beam blocks (concrete blocks with built-in channels for reinforcing bars).

Leave $\frac{3}{8}$-inch mortar joints between the blocks and between the blocks and the basement wall.
◆ Use a hammer and cold chisel to make channels for reinforcing bars in square-ended corner blocks as shown above. Set the blocks in place along the short outer edge of the mortar.

◆ Use a pipe to bend pieces of $\frac{3}{8}$-inch reinforcing bar to 90-degree angles and lay the bars in the channels *(inset)*. Fasten the overlapping ends with tie wire.
◆ Fill the blocks and joints with mortar, troweled off flush with the tops.
◆ Make a platform for the safe from broken block cemented with mortar.

2. Installing the safe.

◆ Bolt vertical $\frac{1}{4}$- by 3-inch angle irons to each side of the safe *(page 56)*, $7\frac{1}{2}$ inches in from the front, or have the dealer weld them on.
◆ With a helper, set the safe on the mortar bed.
◆ Lay courses of block behind the safe and along the short edges of the enclosure, leaving $\frac{3}{8}$-inch mortar joints between the courses.

◆ Fill the gaps between the blocks and the safe with mortar, concrete bricks, or concrete half-blocks, depending on the size of the gaps.
◆ Lay a mortar bed or a course of concrete brick, level with the blocks on each side, over the safe, then lay a final course of blocks matching the bottom course *(Step 1)*, but do not fill the blocks with mortar.

3. Reinforcing the blocks.

◆ Bend one end of several reinforcing bars 90 degrees and push the bars down through the cores of the outside blocks as far as possible *(above)*.
◆ Lay horizontal reinforcing bars in the channels around the edges of the top course of blocks *(Step 1)*.
◆ Fill the cores of all the blocks with mortar, then cover the cores with a course of concrete brick.

HOMEMADE STRONGROOMS

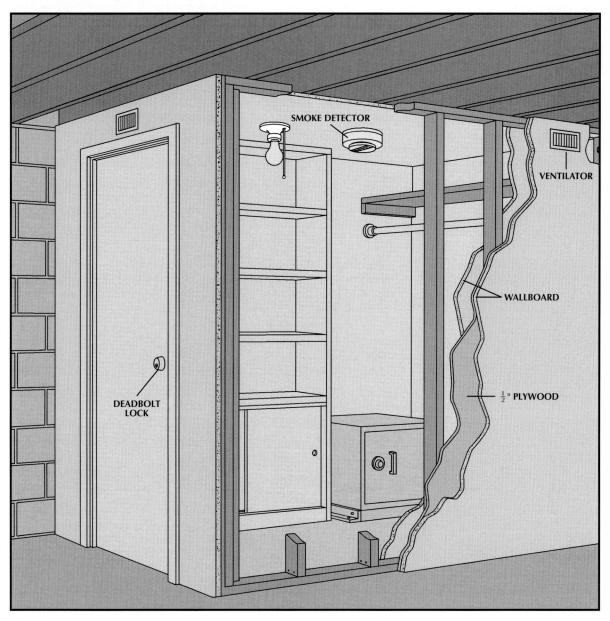

Building a strongroom.

To protect oversize objects—and to provide extra protection for a safe or to keep hazardous items out of a child's reach—you can build a strongroom from scratch *(above)* or convert an existing walk-in closet. Follow these steps:

◆ Working on the outside of a new room or the inside of an existing closet, cover the wall studs with $\frac{1}{2}$-inch plywood nailed every 6 inches.

◆ Add a layer of $\frac{5}{8}$-inch Type X wallboard, nailing it every 8 inches *(pages 91-92)*. Sheathe the ceiling and—in the case of a new room—the other side of the studs with $\frac{5}{8}$-inch wallboard.

◆ Install a $1\frac{3}{4}$-inch solid-core wood flush door that has been reinforced with steel rods *(page 28)*, mounted to swing inward on $4\frac{1}{2}$-inch hinges and fitted with a deadbolt lock *(pages 41-43)* as well as a maximum-security strike *(pages 28-29)*.

◆ Frame holes in two of the walls and install 6- by 8-inch louvered ventilators to prevent moisture from collecting inside the room.

◆ Add a light fixture and smoke detectors, one inside and one outside the room, wired to a centrally controlled alarm system *(pages 64-65)*. A magnetic sensor on the door and an infrared or a microwave sensor inside provide maximum burglar protection.

Silent Sentries, Loud Alarms

Electric alarms that detect intruders, fire, and other dangers were once found only in businesses and the homes of the wealthy. Today, any homeowner can attain a high level of security by installing inexpensive, stand-alone sensors or by equipping the house with an all-seeing central security system that can be monitored by any of several firms specializing in such services.

A window-mounted magnetic sensor →

Self-Contained Warning Systems

A stranger approaches your home while you are away, slips to the side of the house, and starts to raise an unlocked window. A piercing alarm sounds, and the would-be intruder hurries away.

Protecting your home against intrusion need not require an elaborately wired system monitored by a security firm. Just as smoke detectors can give warning of a fire *(pages 86-87)*, screw-on alarms are adequate in low-crime areas.

The models shown here can be bought at hardware and electronic-equipment stores. Make sure to put in fresh batteries when you install

them; then periodically test the devices, and replace the batteries at least once a year.

Choosing the Right Unit: The most common intrusion alarm is a battery-operated protector that buzzes loudly when the door or window is opened *(below)*.

A door-chain alarm *(bottom)* can be set to sound only while you are inside the house. It makes enough noise to alert you and to frighten off most potential intruders, but one who stays long enough to see where the noise is coming from can silence the alarm simply

by flicking the ON/OFF switch.

More difficult to silence is the model opposite, which is set with a removable key. Although it is more costly, it also comes with a special disarming switch that lets you turn the protector on, then come and go without tripping the alarm.

A Canine Guardian: Many homeowners rely on a family dog to alert them in case of fire or burglars—and some security consultants consider a dog the best protection of all. Follow the advice on the opposite page to find a puppy suitable for both protection and family life.

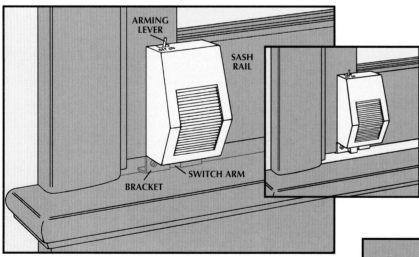

A window buzzer.
◆ With the window open, push the prongs on the unit's bracket up into the bottom rail of the lower window sash, then stick the bracket in place, using its adhesive backing strip.
◆ Close the window and set the arming lever to ON *(left)*. The pressure of the window sill retracts a spring-loaded switch arm. If an intruder raises the window *(inset)*, the switch arm is released and the alarm sounds.

A door-chain alarm.
◆ Mount the battery-powered alarm unit at the edge of the door about 18 inches above the doorknob.
◆ Set the chain knob at the center of the alarm slot, then position the chain bracket on the doorframe so that there is about $\frac{1}{2}$ inch of slack in the chain when the door is closed. Mount the bracket.
◆ Turn the unit on *(right)*. When the door is opened, the chain pulls its knob to the side of the alarm slot. The knob then presses two electrical contacts together so that the alarm is activated and the buzzer sounds.

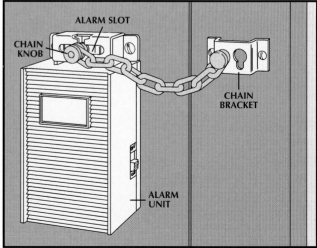

A locking door alarm.

Alarms vary, but the one shown at right is typical.

◆ Mount the alarm unit 18 inches above the doorknob and about $\frac{1}{8}$ inch from the edge of the door.

◆ Position the magnetic sensor at the edge of the doorframe, $\frac{1}{4}$ inch below the top of the unit. The alarm sounds when contact is broken between the magnetic sensor in the alarm unit and the one on the doorframe.

◆ Turn on the alarm with the key and confirm that the indicator light is on.

◆ When everyone is in for the night, set the disarming switch to IN. The buzzer will sound if the door opens.

◆ To leave the house, move the switch to OUT. This gives an occupant 30 seconds to walk out the door and close it; if the door stays open longer, the buzzer will sound. Similarly, you can unlock and reenter the house without sounding an alarm, provided you do not leave the door open more than 30 seconds.

◆ While the alarm is on, use the cutoff button when you answer the door to keep the buzzer silent.

◆ Whenever the buzzer sounds, it will continue to do so until turned off with the key.

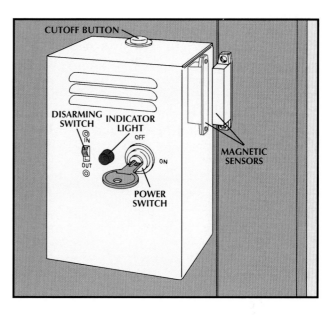

THE ULTIMATE ALARM—A FAMILY DOG

Perhaps the most reliable security system is a living one—the family dog. Self-contained, requiring neither electricity nor installation, it can be trained to respond to most dangers or threats of danger. Most dogs will raise an alarm in response to intrusion or fire, but differences in temperament make some better watchdogs than others.

A dog with a very submissive temperament, for example, may hesitate to bark at intruders. An extremely dominant dog, on the other hand, is not suited to a house with small children and can pose challenges to an inexperienced owner. Look for a dog with a personality between these two extremes. If you are interested in a puppy, ask an experienced breeder or dog trainer to assess its personality for you, a process that is known as puppy testing. You can often gauge the personality of an adult dog for yourself, but advice from a trainer or an experienced animal-shelter worker can help you match your house and family with the appropriate dog.

Once you have taken home a puppy or new dog, it will need only obedience training and loving care to develop the combination of qualities that make a good family watchdog. You can train a dog yourself at the obedience classes offered in many areas or with the help of one of the number of books available on the subject.

Further protection training is unnecessary for family pets. Dogs that go beyond the sounding of an alarm to attack intruders are not recommended as family pets, although some people living alone prefer aggressive "one-man" dogs. A dog trained to bite any hand that holds a weapon or attack any suspicious person is generally advisable only to protect commercial property.

A central security system offers far better protection for an entire house than stand-alone alarms. Consisting of an interconnected network of sensors and sirens, such a system is more versatile and easier to maintain than a collection of separate alarms because you can control everything from a single point.

There are two basic types of central systems: hard-wired, in which each sensor is connected to a main control box with wires, and wireless, with battery-powered sensors that communicate with the control box by radio signal. Additionally, some systems combine hard-wired and wireless technologies. Equipment for each type can be found at any alarm-equipment distributor.

Hard-Wired Systems: In this set-up, the control box plugs into a standard wall outlet through a transformer, which steps the standard 120-volt household service down to between 16 and 20 volts. By sending a small current through the wires, the control box continuously monitors each sensor and sounds the alarm if any of them is tripped. To provide backup in case of a power failure, a battery must also be connected to the system.

Most systems are activated and deactivated through wall-mounted keypads *(page 81)*, one typically located at the main entrance to the house and another in the master bedroom. The keypads allow you to turn the system on when you leave the house, off when you return, and back on again when you go to bed.

Wireless Systems: In homes where fishing wires is unusually difficult, the solution is to install a wireless system *(page 82)*, in which typically only the keypads are wired to the control box. Wireless sensors, although much easier to install than hard-wired components, are more expensive, and you must periodically replace the batteries that run them.

The Sensors: Both hard-wired and wireless systems offer a variety of sensors to protect every part of a home. The first line of defense are the contact sensors at each door and window *(pages 73-75)*. When the system is armed, these sensors trigger the alarm whenever a door or window is opened. And to alert the system when an intruder breaks a windowpane, special glassbreak detectors set off the alarm at the sound of shattering glass.

The second line of defense consists of interior sensors *(pages 77-78)*, which detect the presence of an intruder who somehow manages to get into the house undetected. The most common of these is the passive infrared sensor, which responds to heat that is emitted by the human body. Other interior sensors discern motion either as a disturbance in a field of low-energy radiation (microwave) or as an interruption of a light beam (photoelectric). Still others combine passive infrared and microwave technologies to create a heat-and-motion sensor.

Finally, smoke detectors are recommended for all central systems. Types of devices are described and placement suggestions are given on pages 86 and 87.

Alarm Options: For added peace of mind, you can contract with a local security company to monitor your alarm system. Through an automatic telephone dialer in the control box, the company receives a signal when the alarm goes off. Things to look for in a security company appear on page 72.

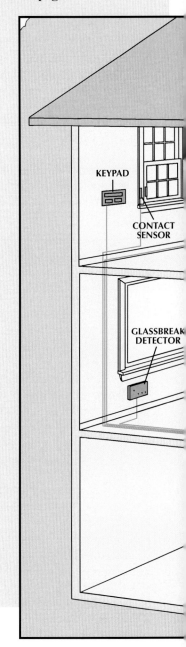

KEYPAD

CONTACT SENSOR

GLASSBREAK DETECTOR

A hard-wired alarm system.

In the house that is shown below, each element of the security system is individually wired to a control box in the basement. The exterior doors have contact sensors, and windows accessible from the ground or the deck atop the garage have both contact sensors and glassbreak detectors. Inside the house, passive infrared detectors check for the telltale heat signature of an intruder. Smoke detectors are located at key points throughout the house: the upstairs hall, the bedroom, the workshop, and the basement stairwell. Both the kitchen and the bedroom are equipped with keypads, and the bedroom contains a panic button for triggering the alarm in case of an emergency.

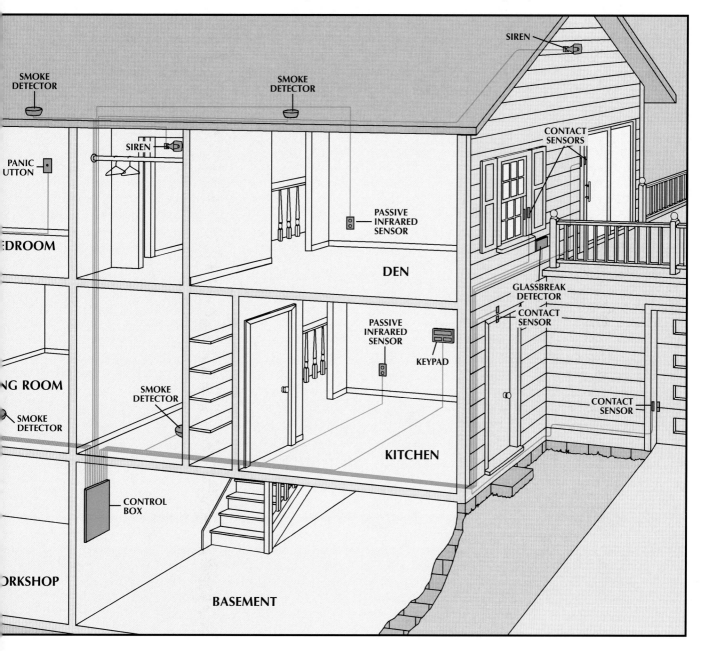

The electrical codes that cover low-voltage wiring allow you to fish security system cable behind baseboards and in other places you cannot run standard household wiring. The guidelines below and on the pages that follow are designed to let you hard-wire your entire house with a minimum of difficulty.

The Wire: Most security systems use 18- to 22-gauge cable with stranded wires, available at most home-supply stores. Some components call for two-conductor cable, others for up to five-conductor cable; the manufacturer's instructions will specify which type to buy. To figure out how much cable you will need, first estimate the total distance from each element to the control box. Then add 20 percent to that figure, since cables rarely run in a straight path. Finally, add an extra foot for each component in the system, to allow for making the connections.

The Path of Least Resistance: In most houses, the simplest wiring route is through an unfinished attic or basement. Start by running the cable through the unfinished room to a location directly above or below the alarm component. Use a staple gun with a wiring attachment to secure a cable along exposed joists; if you need to cross joists, drill a $\frac{3}{8}$-inch hole through the center of each joist and string the cable through it.

Next, make the short run through the inside of a wall from the unfinished room to the alarm component. The tools required for this task include springy steel fish tapes and a long string or chain—both used for pulling cable through walls—and a long electrician's extension bit for your drill. A straightened wire coat hanger may come in handy for pushing insulation out of the way in an exterior wall.

Wiring Shortcuts: Usually, the wiring of a security system will require at least one long vertical run between attic and basement. Since every house has at least one plumbing stack running from the basement to the roof, the excess space along this stack *(page 67)* offers an excellent route.

Closets on successive levels of a house can also provide a handy vertical path. If the closets are stacked directly over each other, drill through the ceiling of one into the floor of the next. If they are offset, you may be able to fish cable a short distance through a joist space shared by the closets *(page 68)*; alternatively, you can run cable out of the top of a lower closet to a molding, then into the bottom of an upper closet.

When running cable through closets or unfinished rooms is impossible, look for other ways to avoid long, tricky fishes through walls. Tuck and staple cable along the edges of wall-to-wall carpets (a crochet hook to lift the edge of the carpet is sometimes helpful), or hide it behind baseboards, chair rails, moldings, or door and window casings. You can also hide cables under rugs or carpeting, but be sure to avoid places where the insulation could be damaged or the wires broken by foot traffic or furniture.

Making Connections: To guarantee secure, long-lasting connections between two wires, or between wires and components, solder them *(pages 70-71)*. An inexpensive soldering iron with a 25- to 50-watt heating element will serve, though a soldering gun can speed the job. Whichever tool you choose, sandpaper the pieces to be connected before beginning the job, and be sure to use rosin-core electrical solder: The acid core in plumbing solder would weaken a connection. After soldering, wrap the exposed wires tightly with electrician's tape.

 TOOLS

Electric drill
Flexible drill bit
Fish tapes
Chain
Fishing weight
Magnet
Staple gun with
   wiring attachment
Wire hanger
Crochet hook
Wood chisel
Hammer
Cold chisel
Utility knife
Soldering iron or
   gun
Long-nose pliers

 **MATERIALS**

18-gauge cable
Rosin-core solder
Electrician's tape
Wire cap
Staples

 **SAFETY TIPS**

Wear safety glasses to protect your eyes when stapling, drilling, and chiseling. When using an electric drill in a cramped space, reduce the noise with earplugs.

WIRING FROM A BASEMENT OR ATTIC

1. Drilling from below.

◆ In a room above the basement, bore a small location hole through the floor, just outside the wall space through which you will pull cable. Stick a scrap of stiff wire through the hole in order to mark the position of the hole.

◆ From the basement, find the marker wire and drill up through the sole plate of the wall with a long bit *(right)*. If you are working near the foundation wall, you may have to angle the bit to hit the plate.

When running cable from the attic down to a finished room, follow the same procedure in reverse: Drill the location hole up through the room's ceiling, then drill through the top plate of the wall from the attic.

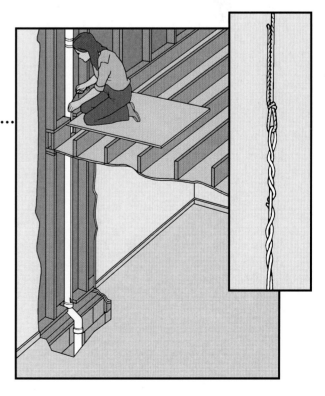

2. Fishing the cable.

◆ From the position of the component, drill a hole through the doorframe or window frame—or through the nearest wall stud, in the case of an interior sensor or keypad—and push the end of a fish tape through it into the wall.

◆ Have a helper push a second tape through the hole drilled in the wall plate and maneuver both tapes until their ends catch *(left)*. In an exterior wall filled with insulation, use the natural curl of the fish tape to keep it between the inside face of the wallboard and the vapor barrier of the insulation.

◆ Pull the hooked tapes into the basement or attic, unhook them, attach the cable to the tape leading from the component's position, and pull the cable through the wall.

ROUTING CABLE BETWEEN WALLS

Wiring along a stack vent.

◆ From the attic, lower a small fishing weight attached to a long piece of string or chain into the space alongside the plumbing stack. If the weight is blocked, jiggle and bounce it until it falls past the obstruction.

◆ When the string reaches the basement, attach cables to the string, staggering the points of attachment to avoid a bulky connection *(inset)*.

◆ Pull the string and cables back up through the stack.

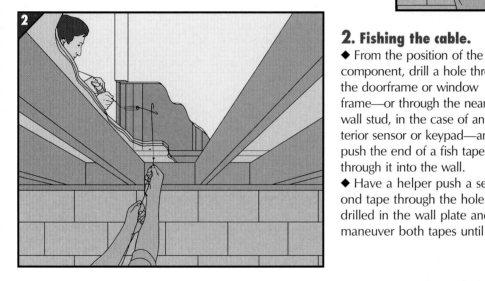

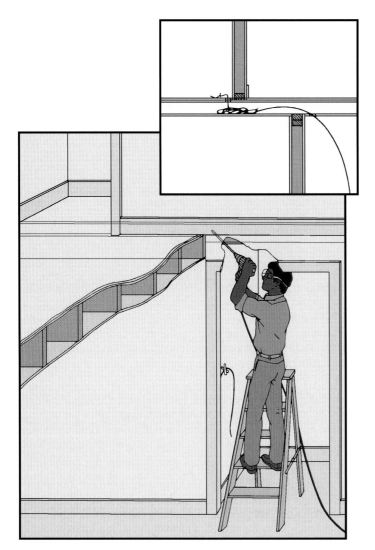

Wiring through closets.

Use the following procedure when closets are not stacked directly above one another:

◆ Fish cables from the basement through a hole drilled in the floor of a closet above.

◆ Drill a hole through the closet ceiling into the space between the joists above.

◆ Drill a hole down into the same joist space through the floor of a closet on the next floor.

◆ Tack one end of a heavy string to the floor of the upper closet. Wrap the other end into loops, and stuff the loops down into the joist space.

◆ Push a fish tape through the hole in the lower closet and snag the string *(inset).* Pull the string into the lower closet, tie it to the cables, and pull them into the upper closet.

If the closets do not share a joist space, remove a section of baseboard in an upper room and drill behind it on an angle into the joist space above the lower closet. Fish cables through and run them behind the baseboard *(below)* to the nearest closet or sensor.

RUNNING CABLE IN A FINISHED ROOM

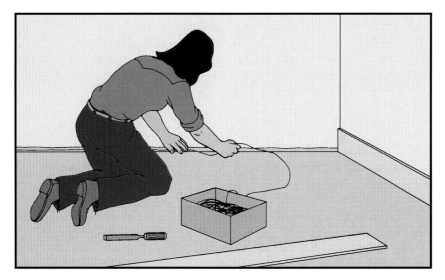

Hiding cable behind baseboards.

◆ Insert the blade of a wood chisel between the wall and the top of the baseboard and, working from one end of the baseboard to the other, carefully pry it away from the wall.

◆ Push the cable into the gap between the floor and the bottom of the wallboard, stapling it in place if necessary. If there is no gap, cut a groove for the cable along the wall; use a utility knife to cut away wallboard and a hammer and cold chisel for plaster.

◆ Nail the baseboard back in place, angling the nails to avoid the cable.

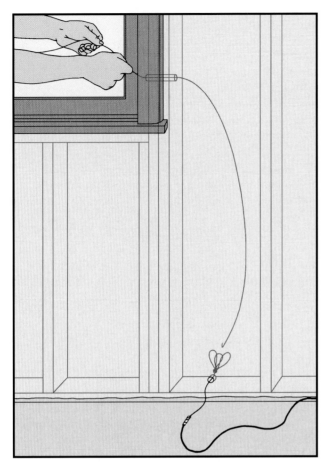

Fishing cable from behind a baseboard.
◆ Tie one end of a piece of string into a series of loops, and tie the other end to the alarm cable.
◆ Below the sensor location, drill a hole in the wall behind the baseboard, and push the string loops through.
◆ Push a fish tape through the sensor hole and catch the string loops with it *(left)*. Then pull the tape, string, and cable through the sensor hole.

TRICKS OF THE TRADE

Fishing Cable with a Magnet

Instead of using a looped string and fish tape to run cable down along a wall *(above)*, it is often easier to do the job with a magnet and a length of nonrigid ferromagnetic chain. Simply drop the chain through the sensor hole into the wall and draw it out the exit hole at the base of the wall with the magnet *(right)*. Then tie the cable to the chain and pull it through the sensor hole. You can buy chain-and-magnet sets at an electrical-supply shop, or fashion your own.

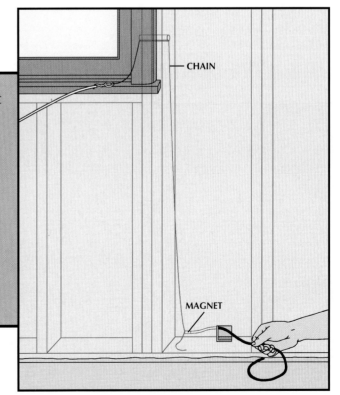

CHAIN

MAGNET

A DRILL BIT THAT GOES AROUND CORNERS

If you need to make many short wiring runs from door or window sensors to spaces below or above, you can save time by purchasing a flexible drill bit like the one shown at right. Available in lengths of $4\frac{1}{2}$ and 6 feet, the bit has a flexible, spring-steel shaft with a small hole in each end. These features make it possible to drill through walls, then attach wires to the bit and pull them through the hole as you withdraw the bit.

For best results, use the bit with a variable-speed reversible drill. First bore a hole halfway through the jamb at the sensor's location with a regular bit, angling the hole toward the attic or basement. Then complete the hole with the flexible bit. When you feel the bit emerge from the studs of the rough frame, stop the drill and slide the bit forward until it strikes the next stud, which will deflect it up or down to the wall plate. Then drill through the plate.

Fish the wires with a device called a wire basket, consisting of a net and a swiveling hook that attaches to the hole in the bit *(inset)*. To link the cable to the basket, push the cable into the net; as you pull on the cable, the net pulls tight around it. The swivel hook allows you to run the drill—sometimes necessary to pull the bit back out of the holes—without twisting the wires.

Flexible bits and wire baskets are available at electrical- and alarm system-supply houses. Other helpful accessories include alignment handles and guide tubes to bend the bit into tight curves, and extensions that allow you to drill as far as 10 feet.

MAKING WIRE CONNECTIONS

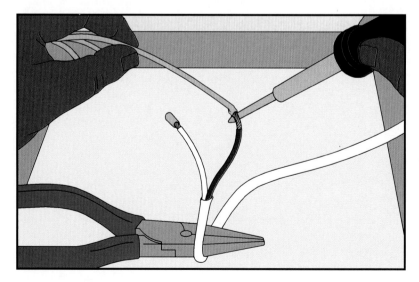

Tinning a lead.
◆ Strip $\frac{3}{4}$ inch of insulation from the lead and twist the strands of wire together tightly.
◆ Hold the soldering iron to the wire for a few seconds to heat it thoroughly.
◆ Touch the solder to the heated wire—not to the iron—and let it flow evenly over the lead *(left)*. The solder should begin to flow almost instantly; if it does not, remove the solder, heat the wire a little longer, and try again.

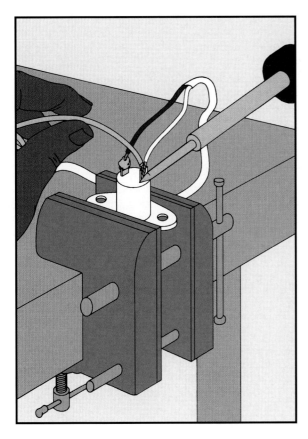

Soldering a wire to a tab.
◆ Pull the tinned end of the wire through the hole in the tab with long-nose pliers and wrap the wire in a loop around the tab.
◆ Heat the tab on one side and dab enough solder on the other side to cover the joint smoothly.

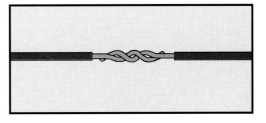

Soldering wires together.
◆ Expose about $\frac{3}{4}$ inch of each wire and wrap them around each other as shown above.
◆ Heat the wire joint with a soldering iron, then touch the solder to the wires until the joint is evenly covered with solder.
◆ Cover the joint completely with electrician's tape.

MAKING CONNECTIONS WITH WIRE CAPS

As an alternative to soldering, you can splice cable with wire caps specially made for thin, low-voltage wires. Though not as strong as soldered joints, such splices will serve in tight spots where soldering is difficult.

To use the caps, strip about $\frac{1}{2}$ inch of insulation from the end of each wire, twist the ends together, and then insert the exposed wire into the cap. With pliers pinch the cap flat; this causes the metal teeth within the cap to clamp down on the wires. Finally, wrap the entire connection with electrician's tape.

Elements of a Home-Security System

The following pages describe how to install the parts of a hard-wired or wireless home-security system.

Full Coverage: It is vital to have a sensor at every point of entry easily accessible to an intruder. The most widely used sensors for doors and windows are the two-piece magnetic type *(pages 73-75)*, though they will not suffice for the entire house.

Among other useful sensors are bars equipped with mercury switches to protect tilting windows *(page 76)*, electronic glassbreak detectors that sound the alarm if someone tries to break the glass in a door or window *(page 76)*, and special screens that allow you to open a window while the system remains armed *(page 77)*.

But no matter how well protected the perimeter of the house, it is important to install sensors inside the house in case someone manages to gain entry. The major types of interior sensors work by detecting heat, motion, or both *(pages 77-78)*.

The Rest of the System: In addition to the control box, to which all the elements of the security system are wired, you will need at least one siren. The types available are illustrated on page 80.

Added security comes from smoke detectors *(pages 86-87)*, as well as heat sensors that detect dangerous rises in room temperature *(page 78)*. And a panic button *(pages 79-80)*, which sets off the alarm at a touch, provides still greater peace of

mind. Once all the devices are in place, you must mount the keypads, through which you give the system its instructions *(page 81)*.

How to Proceed: First determine which components you need and where to place them around the house. If the component is wireless you can simply screw it in place, but if it is hard-wired you must then fish its wires to the control box *(pages 66-70)*. Connect the wires to each component—either by screwing them to terminals on the device or by soldering them to leads on the device *(pages 70-71)*—and secure the component in place. Finally, connect all the wires to the control box and attach the transformer and backup battery *(pages 81-82)*.

 TOOLS

Electric drill
Soldering gun
Screwdriver
Hammer
Electronic stud finder
Keyhole dry-wall saw
Pliers

 **MATERIALS**

Glue
Rosin core solder
Electrician's tape
Low-voltage cable

SAFETY TIPS

Safety goggles protect your eyes when you are hammering and working with power tools.

CALLING FOR HELP

The best protection for your home is provided by local police and fire departments. To notify them when your alarm goes off, hire a security company to monitor your system. Whenever a sensor is tripped, an automatic telephone dialer installed in the control box contacts the company, which alerts the fire department if a smoke or heat detector has gone off, and the police if any other element has caused the alarm. To guard against false alarms, a security-company employee calls your house and asks for a preestablished password. If nobody answers the phone—or an incorrect password is offered—the proper authorities are dispatched.

If you install your own security system, the monitoring company will probably want to inspect your work. A reputable company will display the seal of the National Burglar and Fire Alarm Association *(above, right)*, which trains security professionals throughout the country.

NATIONAL BURGLAR & FIRE ALARM ASSOCIATION, INC. Member

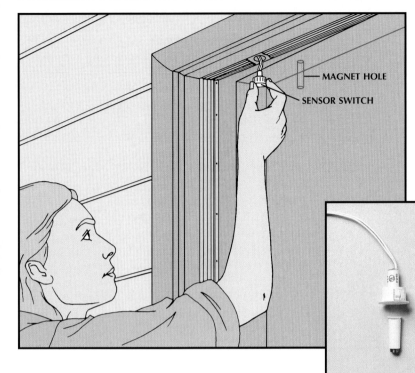

MAGNET HOLE

SENSOR SWITCH

Installing a magnetic sensor.

Install the sensor at any point along the top or latch edge of the door or casement window. For double-hung windows choose a location along the bottom edge of the lower sash or the top edge of the upper sash.

◆ Drill a hole in the edge of the door or window sash to fit the sensor magnet, removing weather stripping if necessary. Opposite this hole, bore another in the frame to fit the sensor switch.

◆ Fish circuit wires through the frame hole and solder them to the switch leads *(pages 70-71)*.

◆ Push the switch into the hole in the frame—as shown in the photograph at left, the switch is ribbed to hold it in place—and glue the magnet into the hole in the door or window sash.

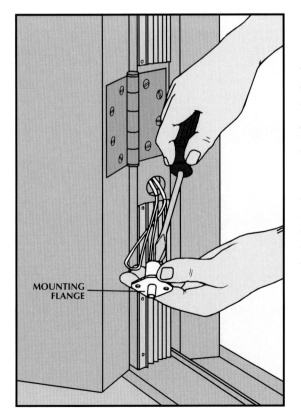

MOUNTING FLANGE

Installing a push-button sensor.

Though not as widely used as magnetic sensors, these devices are useful on double doors.

◆ Drill a sensor hole in the hinge side of the door jamb, removing weather stripping if necessary.

◆ Fish circuit wires and connect them to sensor terminals, then push the wires into the hole and screw the sensor to the jamb through holes in the sensor's mounting flange. Recess the flange into the jamb only if the door fits very tightly.

◆ Test the switch. If there is too large a gap between the door and frame, the door will not push the button in far enough to keep the alarm from tripping. The remedy is to glue a shim to the edge of the door opposite the button.

PROTECTING A DOUBLE-HUNG WINDOW

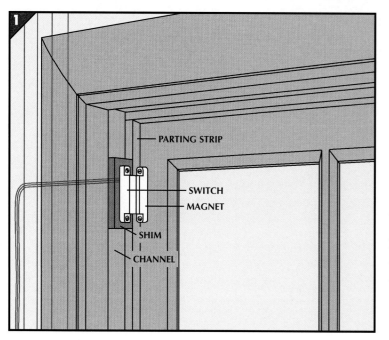

1. Arming the outer sash.
◆ Raise the outer sash to the top of the window frame.
◆ Fasten the magnet of a magnetic-switch sensor *(opposite)* to the edge of the sash, near the top.
◆ Cut a wood shim the same width as the frame's parting strip and slightly longer than the switch. Nail the shim to the frame at the magnet's level.
◆ Lower the sash to provide room to work, and drill a $\frac{3}{8}$-inch hole through the shim, the sash channel, and the adjacent wall studs.
◆ Run circuit wires behind the wall and through the hole.
◆ Connect the wires to the switch, and screw it to the shim so that it barely clears the magnet when you raise the sash *(left)*.

2. Equipping the inner sash.
◆ Raise the inner sash to provide room to work.
◆ At least 4 inches above the window stool, drill a $\frac{3}{8}$-inch hole through the window stop, the jamb, and the studs next to it.
◆ Run circuit wires behind the wall and the casing and out the hole.
◆ Connect the wires to the sensor switch and mount the switch on the stop, next to the sash.
◆ Then close the window and screw the sensor magnet to the sash, alongside the switch *(right)*.

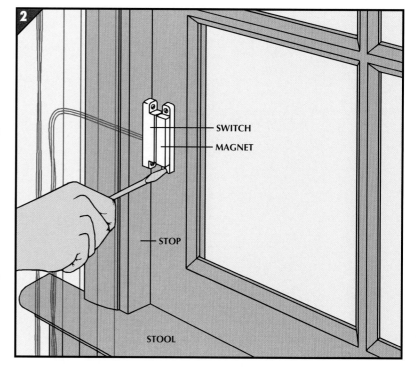

HOW A MAGNETIC-SWITCH SENSOR WORKS

The switch portion of a magnetic sensor contains two metal filaments called reeds. The reeds are encased in a sealed glass tube that helps prevent corrosion, which can lead to false alarms.

When the magnet is near the switch *(below, left)*, it pulls the reeds into contact with each other, completing an electrical circuit that carries a small current from the control box. As the window is opened *(below, right)*, the magnet moves away from the switch. The reeds separate, breaking the circuit and interrupting the current from the control box, which turns on the alarm-system siren and activates the automatic telephone dialer.

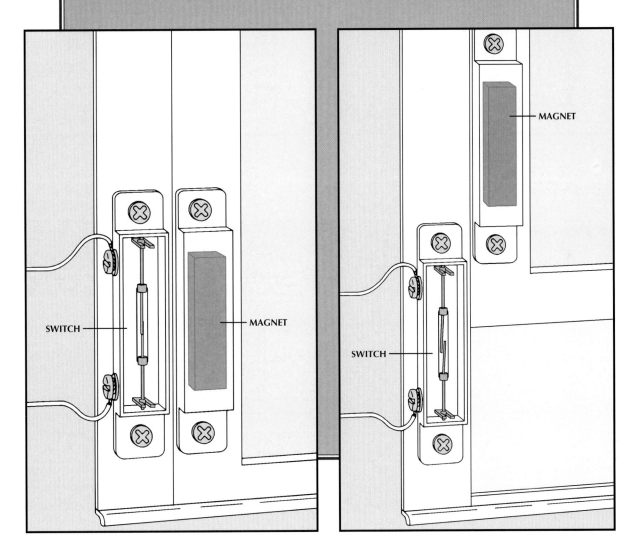

SWITCH — MAGNET — MAGNET — SWITCH —

UNUSUAL SAFEGUARDS FOR WINDOWS

Glassbreak detectors.

These sensors consist of wall boxes that contain sound-analyzing microchips. The most reliable types will trigger the alarm only if they detect two sounds: a low-frequency thump against the glass, followed by the higher frequencies generated when the glass shatters. By waiting for both sounds, the device avoids the false alarms that might result from a bird's flying into a windowpane without breaking it, for example.

Most glassbreak detectors work when mounted within about 15 feet of a window. This wide field of coverage allows you to position a single detector so that it can monitor several windows.

Barrier bars.

Ideal for casement windows and other hinged windows, this device contains a mercury switch concealed in a spring-loaded horizontal bar that you wedge into the window frame. To get into the house, an intruder must push the bar aside, jostling the mercury switch and triggering the alarm. Auxiliary vertical bars slide onto the horizontal bar to make it more difficult for the intruder to overcome this defense by slipping over or under the horizontal bar.

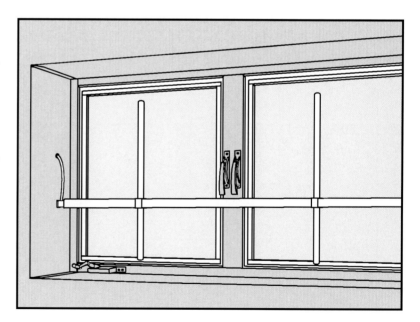

A wired screen.

Set into a window in place of an ordinary screen, this sensor allows you to leave a window open for ventilation while the security system remains armed. Extending from a contact at the bottom of the screen are a series of trigger wires running vertically through the mesh. An intruder cannot cut through the screen without severing at least one of the wires, setting off the alarm. To prevent the intruder from entering by removing the screen, install the switch of a magnetic sensor like the one shown on page 74. Mount the switch on the window frame next to a magnet built into the screen frame.

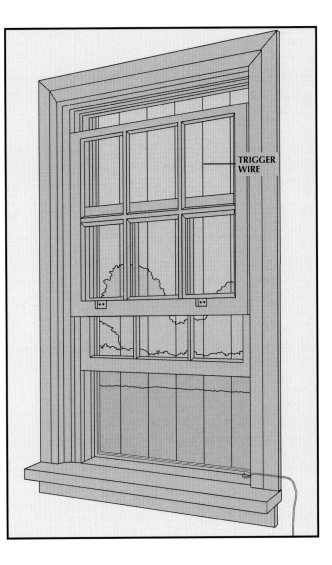

TRIGGER WIRE

EYES FOR THE INTERIOR OF A HOUSE

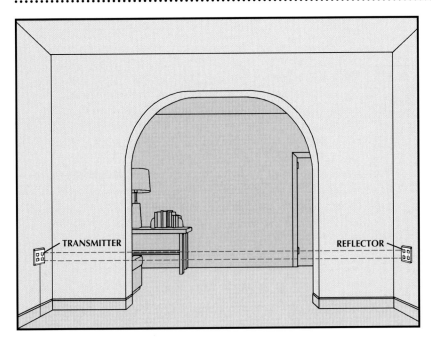

TRANSMITTER

REFLECTOR

A photoelectric detector.

This sensor transmits a beam of light across an entranceway to a reflector on the opposite wall, which directs the beam back to the transmitter. When the beam is interrupted by someone walking across the entranceway, the alarm goes off.

To install this device, you must carefully position the reflector so that it bounces the signal back to the transmitter. The reflector needs no wiring of its own, but the transmitter requires four-conductor cable, which provides the power needed to generate the light beam while keeping the sensor in touch with the control box.

HEAT AND MOTION SENSORS

For a large interior space, passive infrared (PIR) devices usually provide better protection than photoelectric devices, which cover only a narrow area. PIR sensors—a ceiling model appears at near right—detect the presence of infrared energy, or heat. Remarkably sensitive, they are able to distinguish the difference between the amount of heat given off by a person and that emitted by a pet.

More reliable are so-called dual-technology sensors like the wall-mounted model shown at far right. In addition to a heat-sensing PIR element, these devices contain a motion detector—a transmitter that sets up in a room a pattern of low-power microwave radiation, a type of radio signal. The slightest motion disturbs the pattern, alerting the sensor. If both heat and motion occur within a preprogrammed interval—usually a few seconds—the alarm sounds.

PIR and dual-technology sensors, both available in wall- and ceiling-mounted models, look very much alike; read labels carefully when making your selection. Both require at least four-conductor cable; models with built-in tamper switches require six-conductor cable. All models come with reflective foil strips that you can stick inside the device to block the view of a heat source such as a furnace or space heater. Furthermore, you can position the sensors so that they ignore heat or motion in part of a room. The manufacturer's installation instructions explain how to get the coverage you need.

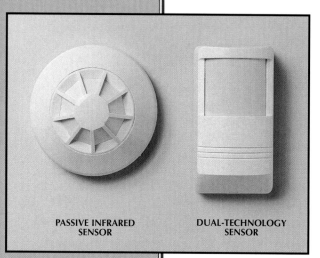

PASSIVE INFRARED
SENSOR

DUAL-TECHNOLOGY
SENSOR

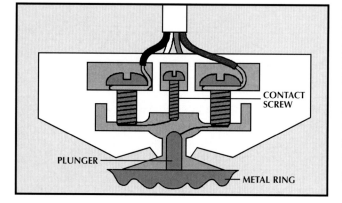

CONTACT
SCREW

PLUNGER

METAL RING

Heat detectors.

Located in a garage or a boiler room, these sensors detect a potentially dangerous buildup of heat. The type illustrated at left, which is wired with four-conductor cable, has a ring of corrugated metal that pops upward at a specific temperature. This action pushes a metal plunger against a contact screw to complete a circuit that sets off the alarm. Typically, heat detectors for rooms with a relatively low average temperature are built to activate at 135°F. Models for rooms with a higher average temperature respond at 200°F.

1. Cutting the opening.

This procedure calls for an electrical box without built-in mounting brackets.

◆ Identify a spot on the wall, between studs, for an outlet box that will house the panic button. Find the studs with an electronic stud finder.

◆ Hold the back of the outlet box against the wall in the desired location and outline it with a pencil.

◆ Drill a $\frac{3}{8}$-inch hole in each corner of the outline *(left)*.

◆ Cut away the area inside the outline with a keyhole dry-wall saw, using the corner holes to insert and turn the blade.

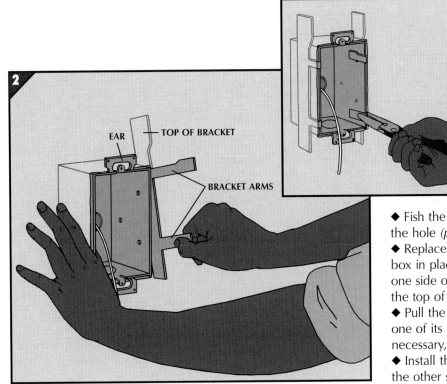

EAR — TOP OF BRACKET

BRACKET ARMS

2. Installing a wall box using brackets.

◆ Place the box in the hole and adjust the ears, if necessary, to make the box flush with the wall surface. Then remove the box.

◆ Fish the necessary wires from the control box to the hole *(pages 66-70)*, and then into the box.

◆ Replace the box in the hole. While holding the box in place, slip a bracket into the wall between one side of the box and the edge of the opening. Slip the top of the bracket in first, then the bottom *(left)*.

◆ Pull the bracket against the inside of the wall by one of its arms, then bend the arms into the box. If necessary, use pliers to make a tight bend *(inset)*.

◆ Install the second bracket in the same manner on the other side of the box.

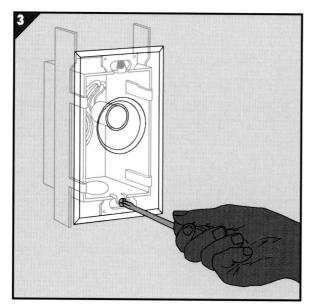

3. Hooking up the panic button.

◆ Connect the wires from the control box to the wire leads of the panic button *(pages 70-71)*.
◆ Mount the panic button and the cover plate to which it is attached onto the outlet box with the screws provided *(left)*.

ALARMS AND SIRENS

Security experts recommend that you install one siren inside the house, in or near a bedroom, and another on an exterior wall of the house or in an attic near a gable vent. Sirens for outdoor use are weatherproof and are unlikely to be disabled or to sound a false alarm because of rain or snow. Many sirens are also booby-trapped to go off if any attempt is made to disable them. Tamper-resistant alarms require four-conductor cable, instead of the two-conductor cable used to deliver power to sirens without such a safeguard.

If you live in a townhouse or in a neighborhood where the homes are clustered tight, install a siren with a flashing light *(below, center)*. Located on an exterior wall, the light will eliminate confusion as to the source of the alarm among police or firefighters arriving on the scene.

Many localities require that the control box have an automatic cutoff to silence an exterior siren after a specific amount of time—usually 10 minutes. This feature prevents the device from blaring indefinitely if it should go off while you are away from the house. Once the siren shuts off, the system automatically rearms itself, bypassing the device that originally tripped the alarm.

While sirens for outside or attic use are large, horn-shaped devices, the ones for indoor use are designed to be as unobtrusive as possible. The unit shown below, left, for example, is flush mounted in the wall; it protrudes only about $\frac{1}{2}$ inch.

FLUSH-MOUNTED SIREN   SIREN WITH LIGHT   OUTDOOR SIREN

A KEYPAD COMMAND CENTER

The keypad.

Wired with four-conductor cable—two conductors provide power, the other two allow for communication with the control box—the keypad displays the status of the system at all times. Colored lights let you know if the system is armed or deactivated, and more specific information—such as which sensors have been tripped when the alarm goes off—appears on the display panel. A set of buttons, hidden by a flip-down cover, let you arm and disarm the system by entering a code. Many keypads also act as panic buttons; pressing the star and pound keys sets off the alarm on this model.

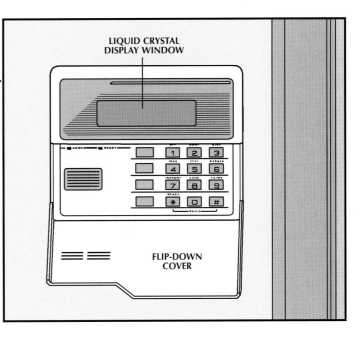

CONNECTING THE CONTROL BOX

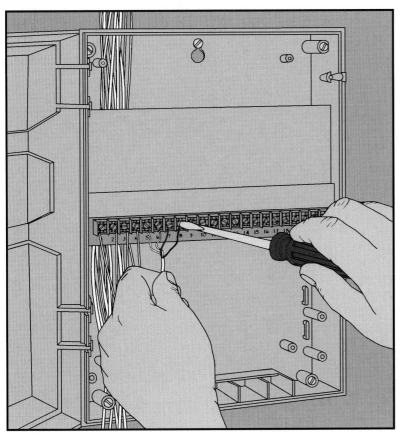

Wiring the box.

Most control boxes use a wiring scheme similar to the one illustrated at left. Each conductor from every cable is connected to a strip of screw terminals. The manufacturer will specify which terminals serve each kind of security-system device. Typically, spaces are reserved for cables coming from the sirens, the keypad, and the smoke and heat detectors. Furthermore, there are terminals on the strip dedicated to devices that are tripped when a circuit is broken—called normally open devices—and those tripped when a circuit is made—called normally closed. For large systems, you can buy and install additional strips. To make it easier to maintain and service the system, label each cable to indicate which sensor it serves.

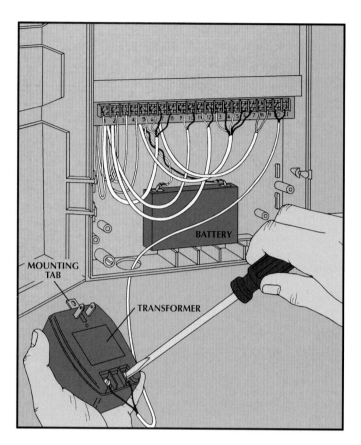

MOUNTING
TAB

TRANSFORMER

BATTERY

Wiring the transformer and battery.

If your box comes with a pair of battery leads already connected to the back of the terminal strip *(left)*, attach the positive and negative leads to the positive and negative ends of the battery. Otherwise, the terminal strip will have positive- and negative-labeled screws from which you can run wires to the battery.

To wire the transformer to the box, connect its two wire leads to the screws on the terminal strip identified for this purpose. Before plugging it into a receptacle, first remove the screw for the receptacle's cover plate. Hold the cover plate in place, plug the transformer into the receptacle, and reset the cover plate screw so that it goes through the mounting tab on the transformer. At this point, the system is ready for use.

A WIRELESS SECURITY SYSTEM

A wireless sensor.

Every sensor available for a hard-wired system has a wireless counterpart. Each communicates with the control box by way of a small battery-powered radio transmitter instead of wires fished throughout the house. The diagram at right illustrates the inside of the wireless version of the magnetic switch shown on page 74. When aligned with the same kind of magnet used with a hard-wired switch, reeds touch to close a circuit, preventing the transmitter from broadcasting. When the magnet is moved away, the reeds separate to open the circuit and activate the transmitter. Power for both the circuit and the radio transmitter comes from a 3-volt lithium battery, which lasts from 3 to 5 years. You must still hard-wire sirens and keypads to the control box. The transformer and backup battery are wired to the box as they are in a hard-wired system *(page 81 and above)*.

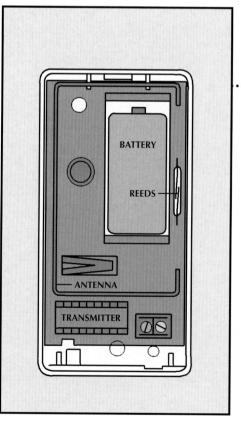

BATTERY

REEDS

ANTENNA

TRANSMITTER

ACCESSORIES FOR A WIRELESS SYSTEM

Wireless components operate on what is called a "supervised" network, in which each element maintains contact with the control box by means of a unique radio signal. If a portable device such as a wireless keypad or panic button is taken out of radio range, for example, or if the batteries in a sensor run down, the box notes the loss of signal and sends an alert through the keypad display.

Though wireless systems have drawbacks—they are more expensive than hard-wired ones and require periodic battery changes—they allow you great freedom. The wireless keypad *(right, top)*, for example, provides you with total access to the system from inside the house. The key ring controller *(right, center)* functions in a similar manner, though its abilities are much more limited. And while both can be used as panic buttons, you can also purchase a remote panic button *(right, bottom)*, which works both inside and outside the house.

WIRELESS KEYPAD

KEY RING CONTROLLER

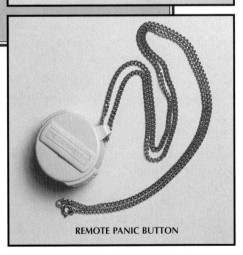

REMOTE PANIC BUTTON

Defenses against Fire

Building and electrical codes make new houses relatively fireproof. Yet no home possesses all the features that can reduce the chance of fire, slow its spread, and ensure escape should fire break out. Taking the steps on the following pages—hanging flame-retarding wallboard, adding firestops, and installing smoke detectors and fire extinguishers—can fill fire-safety chinks that codes don't often address.

Smoke Detectors

Although they are small and inexpensive, smoke detectors can play a priceless protective role. If properly located, they will sound an alarm early enough to enable you to escape from a fire.

Different Sensing Methods: Smoke detectors come in two forms: In a chamber of the ionization type of detector, electrically charged particles flood a gap between two terminals. Normally the particles carry current, but smoke from a fire disrupts the flow and triggers the alarm. In a photoelectric detector, the alarm is tripped when smoke deflects a beam of light onto a light-sensitive switch.

Ionization detectors respond quickly to smoke from clean-burning fires of paper and wood. However, they tend to sound false alarms when exposed to ordinary household fumes and kitchen smoke.

Photoelectric detectors respond slowly to clean-burning fires but quickly to the slow-burning, smoldering fires that occur most frequently in houses—those that produce heavy smoke and are most likely to start in a kitchen, basement, bedroom, or living room.

Battery Backup: Although some detectors operate on the house's electrical current, many models are battery powered and can be installed without difficulty wherever you need them. They also continue to provide protection in the event of a power failure—a likely occurrence in an electrical fire. If your house has hard-wired detectors that lack battery backup, install battery-powered ones next to them.

Most detectors sound a beep when the battery runs low. Even if no low-battery indicator sounds, change the batteries once a year. (An easy-to-remember system is to replace them every autumn when you set back the clock from daylight-saving time.) If you move into a new house or apartment, replace all the batteries at once.

Locating detectors in a house.

Since most fatal fires occur at night, install detectors in hallways outside bedrooms. Some smoke detectors also contain heat sensors, which are useful in furnace rooms, where a rapid rise in temperature can occur before fire breaks out. Install at least one detector on every floor. Set one at the head of a stairwell. Place additional detectors in rooms where fires commonly start; in a kitchen, use a photoelectric model, which will not react to normal cooking fumes. Install extra detectors according to a household's particular circumstances—for example, directly over a sleeping area if that person smokes in bed.

Some communities strictly regulate the placement of smoke detectors. Check with local fire authorities for any special requirements.

SECOND-STORY STAIRS

BEDROOM HALLWAY

LIVING ROOM

KITCHEN

BASEMENT STAIRS

Leave the house immediately. Do not stop to dress, collect valuables, or even call firefighters: Make that call from a neighbor's phone. On the way out, shut doors to retard the progress of flames and smoke.

Avoid smoke if you can. If you cannot, crawl on hands and knees. This keeps you below most of the smoke and carbon monoxide, and above dense toxic gases that settle near the floor.

If your route to safety brings you to a closed door, feel the gaps around the door with the back of your hand before you open it. If the surface is cool, open the door slightly to check for flames or smoke; be ready to slam it shut. If the surface feels hot, do not open the door. Use an alternate escape route.

If you must open a window to escape, first shut all doors to the room. An open door can draw in smoke and flames. If you must break the window, stand back and throw a hard object through it. Clear away glass fragments to prevent cuts as you climb through.

If you are trapped above the ground floor and there is a phone in the room, call the fire department and tell them where you are. Close the door and stuff cloth under it to keep out smoke. Open the window a few inches to breathe. When help arrives, wave your arms or light-colored fabric to attract attention.

If you must escape from the second floor, climb out the window feet first, with your stomach on the sill. Lower yourself as far as possible, then drop, bending your knees when you hit the ground. Drop children to the ground or to a waiting adult before you escape.

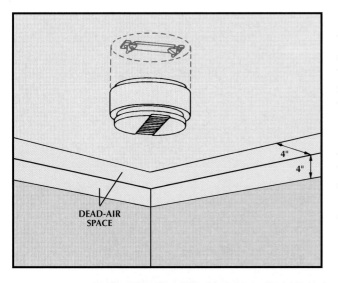

DEAD-AIR SPACE

4"
4"

Locating a detector in a room.

Wherever possible, place a smoke detector at the center of the ceiling. If this location is not practical, observe the following guidelines to avoid dead-air spaces in which the smoke from a fire is unlikely to circulate and a detector will be ineffective:

In most rooms, install a ceiling-mounted detector at least 4 inches from a wall; place a wall-mounted unit no less than 4 inches from the ceiling. In rooms with cathedral or A-frame ceilings, position the smoke detector about 12 inches below the peak of the ceiling. On a beamed ceiling, install the detector on the bottom of a beam, not in the space between beams.

Testing and Maintaining Detectors

Test smoke detectors once a month. Push the test button on a photoelectric model, and test ionization detectors with special aerosol sprays designed for this purpose. If the alarm fails to sound, try a fresh battery. If it still fails, replace the entire detector.

An occasional cleaning prevents dust buildups that can cause a detector to malfunction or to sound false alarms. The upholstery nozzle of a vacuum cleaner is ideal for removing dust or cobwebs. An air blower such as the one at right, available at camera stores, blows dust out of crevices.

Ways to Make a House Hard to Burn

Many homeowners view their defenses against fire mainly in preventive terms, a matter of guarding against such potential causes as an overloaded circuit, grease in an overheated pan, and so on. But because vigilance against fire hazards can never be completely foolproof, a defensive strategy should also embrace containment—ways of making it harder for a fire to spread.

Furnishings: A prudent first step is to take stock of your furnishings. Current consumer-protection laws require all mattresses and carpeting to be made flame resistant, but older mattresses and carpets generally have not been treated. Replace such fire-feeding items.

Walls and Ceilings: The walls of some houses may lack firestops to block the upward spread of fire; a few lengths of 2-by-4 can remedy this situation *(pages 90-91)*. The material of a wall or ceiling will also determine how rapidly fire will spread *(below)*. If a wall or ceiling is finished in a flammable material—or, like some garage walls, not finished at all *(pages 90-92)*—the only good remedy is replacement with safer materials. For extra protection you can use "intumescent" paint, which reacts to the heat of a fire by puffing up into a layer of insulation.

Vegetation: A fire that attacks from outside is more difficult to defend against. But in brush-fire country, such as southern California, there is a way to make a house less likely to burn. Clear easily ignited vegetation from around the house with a scythe and replace it with lawn and fire-resistant plants *(opposite)*.

FIRE RATINGS FOR BUILDING MATERIALS

Flame-Spread Rating	Wall or Ceiling Material
Class A (0–25)—Excellent	Masonry Glass Plaster Type X gypsum wallboard Flame-resistant acoustical ceiling tile Fire-rated fiberboard Asbestos-cement board
Class B (26–75)—Good	Most gypsum wallboard Pressure-treated wood
Class C (76–200)—Fair	Hardboard Particle board Most plywood Most solid wood, 1" thick Most acoustical ceiling tile Fire-rated wall paneling
Class D (over 200)—Poor	Unrated fiberboard Unrated wall paneling

Picking a safe material.

Common coverings for walls and ceilings are grouped into four classes by "flame-spread ratings." Established by the National Institute of Standards and Technology and national testing laboratories, these ratings are based on a comparison of the materials' burning speeds with those of asbestos (specified as 0) and dry red oak (100). Class A and B materials are recommended by fire-prevention experts for halls, stairways, kitchens, and utility rooms. Except in these locations, Class C materials may be used to cover small areas but not an entire room. Class D materials are unsuitable for home use; they do not meet minimum standards of the federal government. Manufacturers of building materials mark many of their products, including acoustical ceiling tiles and wall paneling, with flame-spread ratings.

PLANTINGS FOR BRUSH-FIRE COUNTRY

Type of Plant	Plant Name
Ground Covers	Ice plant *(Drosanthemum hispidum)* Pork and beans *(Sedum rubrotinctum)* Trailing gazania *(Gazania uniflora)* Trailing African daisy *(Osteospermum fruticosum)* Kentucky bluegrass *(Poa pratensis)* Perennial rye grass *(Lolium perenne)* White clover *(Trifolium repens)*
Shrubs	Oleander *(Nerium oleander)* Elephant bush *(Portulacaria afra 'variegata')* Blue chalk sticks *(Senecio serpens)* Toyon *(Heteromeles arbutifolia)* Common lilac *(Syringa vulgaris)*
Trees	Carob *(Ceratonia siliqua)* California pepper *(Schinus molle)* California laurel *(Umbellularia californica)* Cottonwood *(Populus deltoides)*

Common lilac

Selecting the plants.

The foliage plants listed at left are naturally fire resistant—some contain as much as 95 percent water—and all thrive in warm, arid regions where brush fires occur. Plant the yard within 100 feet of the house with ground covers from the chart. Add shrubs and trees for accents, but plant them no closer than 30 feet from the house and no less than 18 feet apart so that a fire cannot jump easily from one to the next and then to the house.

THE POTENTIAL HAZARD OF ALUMINUM WIRING

If your home contains aluminum electrical wiring manufactured and installed in the 1960s or early 1970s, you may have a safety problem. Some aluminum wire produced then had no protective copper coating, leaving it susceptible to two forms of corrosion. These chemical changes increase the wire's resistance to electrical current, which in turn raises the wire's temperature during use—and the potential for an electrical fire.

One type of corrosion results from the joining of two dissimilar metals, as when pure aluminum wiring is attached to standard copper-alloy outlet terminals. A second form of corrosion, oxidation, occurs when aluminum wire is stripped of its insulation and exposed to air.

Corrosion can be prevented if aluminum wiring is installed in exact accord with procedures prescribed by the National Electrical Code. If your house's wiring is pure aluminum—the wires are dull gray and the sheathing is marked AL—all switches, receptacles, and other electrical devices must bear the code CO/ALR. This signifies that the item can safely be used with aluminum wiring as well as copper because it prevents contact between dissimilar metals. Any not marked CO/ALR must be replaced. In addition, exposed aluminum must be covered with a special antioxidizing paste.

As a further precaution, avoid the use of high-wattage appliances in rooms rarely occupied. Also, be aware of warning signs—warm cover plates on switches or outlets, devices that fail to work for no obvious reason, and strange odors or smoke.

⚠️ **CAUTION** *Except for replacing switches or receptacles with ones marked CO/ALR, never attempt to repair or improve an aluminum-wired system yourself. Such work should be undertaken only by a specially trained, licensed electrician.*

Older homes may have a chink or two in their defenses against the spread of fire. Balloon framing, a method of house construction that was common before 1930, has spaces between studs that extend uninterrupted from cellar to roof. Unless blocked by horizontal boards called firestops inside the walls, flames can shoot up these natural chimneys between the studs.

Any house that was built before 1960 with an attached garage may lack a fire-resistant wall to slow a garage fire. A simple fire wall can hold a fire at bay about twice as long as an ordinary wall can.

Identifying Balloon Framing: Shine a flashlight up into the exterior walls from the basement or crawlspace. If you see the bottom of a plywood subfloor but not the wall studs of the story above, your house has

inherently fire-resistant platform-frame construction; each wall has a horizontal board top and bottom, called plates, that serve as firestops.

However, if you can see the wall studs, your house has balloon framing. Use a mirror to reflect a flashlight beam up between the studs, and look in the mirror for firestops. If you see none, you can greatly slow the upward spread of a fire by installing them at the top or bottom of each story *(below and opposite, top)*.

A Garage Fire Wall: Install Type X wallboard on the wall between the garage and the house *(pages 91-92)*. Also add it to a garage ceiling below a living space above.

Designed for fire walls, the gypsum core of Type X wallboard contains, in its crystalline structure, 50 percent water by volume. When heated, the gypsum gradually releas-

es the water as steam, holding back fire for nearly 30 minutes. Adding this material to both sides of the wall can double the protection.

Getting Ready: Check local codes for fire wall requirements such as wallboard thickness. Remove existing wallboard, if any, from the garage wall. Reposition electric switches and receptacles outward as needed to match the thickness of the new wallboard. Also nail strips of lumber to the doorjamb so it will also be flush with the face of the new wallboard.

Finishing the Job: Cover wallboard joints with tape and joint compound. Caulk around any fixtures, ducts, and pipes that pass through the wall. Last, replace the door between the house and the garage with a metal-skin, solid-core, fire-resistant model.

 TOOLS

Circular saw
Hammer
Electric drill with
   screw bit
Keyhole saw
Utility knife
Joint knife
Caulking gun

 **MATERIALS**

2 x 4s
Common nails ($2\frac{1}{2}$"
  and $3\frac{1}{4}$")
Type X wallboard
Dry-wall screws
  ($1\frac{5}{8}$")
Metal pipe strap
Wallboard tape
Joint compound
Caulk

 **SAFETY TIPS**

Protect your eyes from injury with goggles when hammering, sawing, or drilling.

ADDING FIRESTOPS TO A BALLOON-FRAMED HOUSE

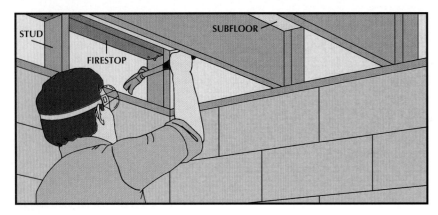

In a basement or crawlspace.
◆ Cut lumber as wide and thick as the studs (usually 2-by-4s) into blocks that fit horizontally between each pair of studs. If joists lie next to studs, cut the blocks to fit between the joists and studs.
◆ Tap the blocks into position—between the studs, the exterior wall, and the edge of the subfloor above—and toenail them to the studs with $3\frac{1}{4}$-inch nails.

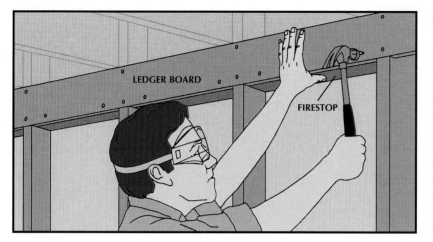

LEDGER BOARD

FIRESTOP

On the first story.
If the first-story studs are exposed during a renovation—or if you are willing to remove and reinstall a strip of the wall covering—nail firestops behind the ledger, or ribbon, board that supports the second-floor joists.
◆ Cut firestops from 2-by-4s to fit between studs and between the exterior wall and the ledger board, which is set into the studs.
◆ Position the firestops as shown at left and drive $2\frac{1}{2}$-inch nails through the ledger board into the blocks.

A FIRE WALL FOR A GARAGE

Installing Type X wallboard.
◆ Mark the center of each stud on the ceiling and floor.
◆ Place a sheet of wallboard against the studs at one end of the wall and push the sheet tight against the ceiling with a foot-operated lever, such as a wedge-shaped piece of wood on a scrap of pipe.
◆ Align the edge of the sheet with the center of a stud and drive several $1\frac{5}{8}$-inch dry-wall screws through the wallboard into the studs to hold the board in place initially *(right)*. Set each screw about $\frac{1}{32}$ inch below the surface and make a gentle depression, or "dimple," around the screwhead, without tearing the paper face of the wallboard.
◆ Remove the lever and drive a pair of screws every 12 inches down each stud, working from the center of the sheet outward. Insert the second screw in each pair 2 inches below the first *(page 92, bottom)*.
◆ Place a single screw every 8 inches around the perimeter of the sheet, about $\frac{3}{8}$ inch from the edges.

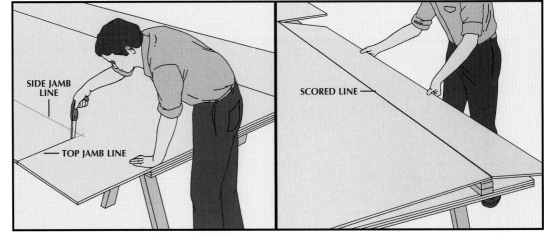

Fitting wallboard around a door.

◆ Measure from the side doorjamb *(page 29, Step 1, inset)* to the edge of the nearest sheet of installed wallboard, and from the ceiling to the top jamb. Transfer these measurements, less $\frac{1}{4}$ inch, to a sheet of wallboard and draw lines to form an outline of the doorway.
◆ Cut the wallboard along the shorter line with a keyhole saw *(above, left)*.

◆ Score the longer line with a utility knife, prop the sheet on two long 2-by-4s as shown above right, and push down abruptly on the edge of the sheet to snap it.
◆ Slice through the backing paper to free the piece, and install the sheet.

Enclosing pipes and ducts.

Frame pipes and ducts running through the wall to provide nailing surfaces for the wallboard.

If a pipe runs through the wall, nail a horizontal 2-by-4 below the pipe to the stud on each side. Toenail a vertical 2-by-4 beside the pipe to the horizontal 2-by-4 and to the top plate of the wall. Fasten the pipe to both 2-by-4s with a bent metal pipe strap *(inset, left)*.

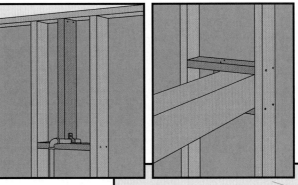

For a duct, nail horizontal 2-by-4s $\frac{3}{4}$ inch above and below the duct. Nail a vertical 2-by-4 between these boards $\frac{3}{4}$ inch from any side not already framed by a stud *(inset, right)*.

◆ Measure from the ceiling to the top and bottom of the pipe or duct and to the centers of the horizontal 2-by-4s. Then measure from the nearest sheet of wallboard to the left and right edges of the pipe or duct and to the center of the vertical 2-by-4s. Transfer all these measurements to a sheet of wallboard, then outline the pipe or duct and the 2-by-4s.
◆ Cut a hole for the pipe or duct with a keyhole saw and cut the wallboard along the centers of the 2-by-4s, so that it will fit around the obstacle like pieces of a jigsaw puzzle.
◆ Screw the larger piece to the wall *(right)*, then the smaller one.

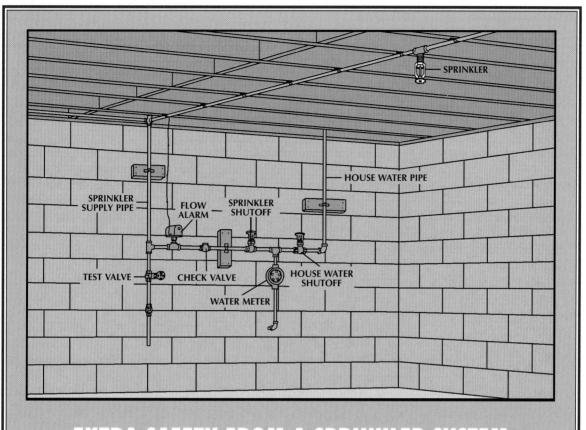

Labels in the diagram:
SPRINKLER
HOUSE WATER PIPE
SPRINKLER SUPPLY PIPE
FLOW ALARM
SPRINKLER SHUTOFF
TEST VALVE
CHECK VALVE
HOUSE WATER SHUTOFF
WATER METER

EXTRA SAFETY FROM A SPRINKLER SYSTEM

A home sprinkler system is made to control or extinguish fires in their early stages, providing a higher level of safety than smoke detectors alone do. When a fire raises the air temperature in a room to a predetermined level— about 160°F—a heat-sensitive element in the sprinkler releases a cover, allowing the sprinkler to soak an area as large as 400 square feet. Usually only one or two sprinklers per room are needed to control a fire.

In a typical system *(above)*, water pipes, fed by the city water line and fitted with sprinklers, run across the ceiling of each story of the house. Sprinklers are available in many styles. The inset at right shows two ceiling models: an inconspicuous flush-mount design for the living spaces of a house *(top)* and a less expensive industrial style for unfinished areas *(bottom)*.

The sprinkler system and the domestic water supply are each controlled by a separate shutoff valve. A backflow check valve keeps sprinkler water out of the domestic water pipes, and a flow sensor sounds an alarm if water moves through the sprinklers. A test valve simulates the discharge of a sprinkler to check the alarm and measure the flow of water.

Some jurisdictions require a sprinkler system if you are building a new home. But even if installation is optional, it is worth considering. Cost is significant, but so are the savings. Most insurance companies offer premium reductions for a professionally installed sprinkler system, and some states offer tax advantages as well.

Portable Extinguishers for Small Fires

Nearly everyone has had an unsettling experience with a minor household fire or the threat of one. Fires in their early stages, however, are often contained in a small space and may be extinguished if attended to quickly.

Quick Solutions: Flames in an oven many times can be put out by closing the door and turning off the heat. A grease fire in a pan can usually be extinguished by sliding a metal cover over the pan and turning off the heat. On an electric stove, move the pan to a cold burner. Do not use water or try to carry a pan of flaming grease outside.

As with grease fires, never use water on an electrical fire. Often you can stop it before it gets well started by pulling the plug or turning off electricity at the service panel.

Water is the best choice, however, on fires in mattresses or cushions. Douse the flames with a pan of water, and when the fire is out, carry the item outdoors and soak it thoroughly.

If your clothes catch fire, roll on the ground or floor to smother the flames—never run. When someone else's clothes are aflame, force the victim down and roll the person over and over. Use a rug, blanket, or coat to help put out the flames. When the fire is out, call an ambulance.

Extinguishers: With a few exceptions, all of these small fires can be put out more safely with fire extinguishers. Do not use an extinguisher on burning grease or burning clothes, however. And if the room is filled with smoke or the fire is fed by plastics or foam rubber—which often produces poisonous fumes—do not attempt to extinguish the fire. In all other cases, if a fire breaks out, alert others to leave the house and to call the fire department, then use an extinguisher *(opposite, bottom)*. If the fire continues to burn after the extinguisher is empty, leave the room, close the door, and wait outside for the firefighters.

Hang fire extinguishers in several locations from hooks screwed to wall studs, and always in the kitchen, garage, and basement. Mount them in plain view near doorways, no more than 5 feet above the floor and as far as possible from spots where a fire is likely to start, such as a stove.

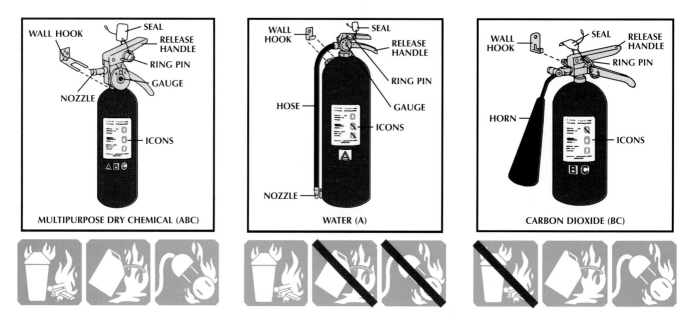

MULTIPURPOSE DRY CHEMICAL (ABC)

WATER (A)

CARBON DIOXIDE (BC)

An arsenal of extinguishers.

Household fires fall into three basic categories: A Class A fire is fed by a solid fuel such as paper or wood; a Class B fire involves a burning liquid such as gasoline or grease; and a Class C fire is one in a live electrical circuit.

Extinguishers—whether containing dry chemicals, water, or carbon dioxide—are labeled with icons representing the classes of fire for which they are intended *(above)*. Each extinguisher has a ring pin or other safety device that immobilizes the release handle to prevent an accidental discharge. A seal, which is easily broken when the ring pin is removed, indicates whether the extinguisher has been used. Check the gauge once a month to see that the canister is fully charged.

Type of extinguisher	Class of fire	Capacity (lbs.)	Range of stream (ft.)	Discharge time (sec.)	Advantages	Limitations
Multipurpose dry chemical	ABC	1–5	5–12	8–10	Can be used on all classes of fires; lightweight; inexpensive.	May not completely extinguish a deep-seated upholstery fire; leaves residue; dry chemical vapor may hamper visibility.
		$2\frac{1}{2}$–9	5–12	8–15		
		9–17	5–20	10–25		
		17–30	5–20	10–25		
Pressured water	A	30	30–40	60	Longer discharge time; greater range.	Must be protected from freezing; initial discharge may create more smoke, hampering visibility.
Carbon dioxide	BC	$2\frac{1}{2}$–5	3–8	8–30	Leaves no residue.	Dissipates in wind; carbon dioxide "snow" may burn skin; eliminates oxygen around immediate area.
		10–15	3–8	8–30		
		20	3–8	10–30		

Selecting an extinguisher.

Use the chart above to select fire extinguishers for your home. For complete protection, you will need more than one type. An extinguisher used against a class of fire for which it is not clearly labeled can actually increase the intensity of the fire.

Multipurpose dry-chemical models, though lighter and less expensive than other kinds, leave behind a powder that is difficult to clean up and that does not work as well against Class A fires as water

does. A water extinguisher, though limited to Class A fires, lets you fight a fire longer and at a safer distance than do other types. Carbon dioxide extinguishers, more costly than dry-chemical or water models, leave no residue.

Buy only those approved by Underwriters Laboratories and at least the size of the smallest units in the chart. Larger units expel their contents at a faster rate to put out a fire quicker, and will put out a larger fire than the smaller units.

ATTACKING THE FLAMES SAFELY

Targeting the fire.

◆ Pull the ring pin from the extinguisher to free the release handle.
◆ At 6 to 8 feet from the fire and with your back to the nearest exit, hold the extinguisher upright and point the nozzle at the base of the flames.
◆ Squeeze the handle and play the stream on the fire, sweeping slowly from side to side, until the fire is out.
◆ Watch the area to make sure the fire does not rekindle, and be prepared to spray again.

Ladders to Escape a House Fire

A quick exit from a burning house requires an early warning and a workable escape plan. Every room should have at least two exits, such as a door and a window. Each family member should know how to leave quickly and safely by every exit.

Family fire drills are necessary to practice climbing through windows, especially windows that are small and relatively inaccessible, such as those in a basement. End each drill at a predetermined meeting spot outside the house so that in a real fire you can tell quickly whether anyone is trapped inside. Post your plan, with exits and the meeting spot clearly marked on a floor plan of the house, and show it to guests and baby-sitters.

For a one-story house such an escape plan, if it is practiced, is generally adequate. In a two- or three-story house a ladder may be needed for an upper-floor window. The ladder can be flexible or rigid, portable or permanently mounted.

Choosing a Ladder: A rigid ladder, permanently fastened to the side of the house, is safest in case of fire, but it can make upper floors accessible to intruders. Such ladders have to be custom-made to match the structure of the house so that they can be attached securely to studs and joists. Usually the professional who makes the ladder also installs it.

Flexible ladders that hang from a window are easily installed, inexpensive, and inconspicuous but somewhat difficult for any but the agile and cool-headed to use in an emergency. Such a ladder should be made of chain or steel cable and fitted with standoff spacers to keep the rungs away from the wall for toe- and handholds.

One type of flexible ladder requires no installation. It is stored near the window, then taken out and hung from the window frame when it is needed *(below)*. Other types are anchored permanently to the floor below a window. The widely used model at right is fitted by the purchaser with a handhold rung and a standoff rung to fit over the window sill.

CABLE-TIED RUNGS TO HANG FROM A WINDOW

CROSS BRACE

SILL HOOK

Using the ladder.
Store the ladder box in an accessible location. When necessary, put the ladder to use as follows:
◆ Remove the lid of the box.
◆ Grasp a sill hook in each hand and pull the hooks out of the box; a spring-and-rod assembly inside a cross brace automatically snaps the hooks together to make a rigid frame.
◆ Drop the rungs out of the window and hook the frame over the sill.
◆ Climb sideways out the window, straddling the sill so that you can see the ladder beneath you, and place your foot on a convenient rung *(left)*.

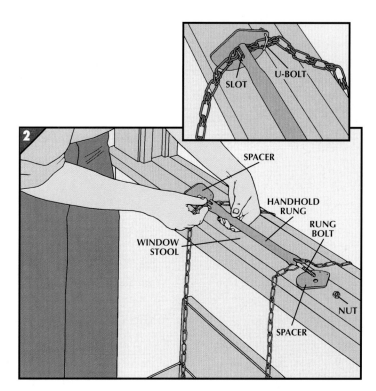

1. Fastening the ladder to the floor.
◆ Slip the end link of each chain through the slot in the center of a floor plate.
◆ Secure the links with curved metal pins provided by the manufacturer *(above)*.
◆ Center the ladder box under the escape window. Then drill through the holes in the bottom of the box to bore pilot holes in the floor for lag screws provided with the ladder.
◆ Put a washer on each lag screw and fasten the floor plates and box to the floor with the screws.

2. Attaching the handhold rung.
◆ Before installing the top two rungs—the rest of the ladder comes preassembled—lower the ladder from the window.
◆ Place the handhold rung between two chain links that lie opposite each other on the interior part of the window sill, which is called the stool. Pass a rung bolt through a small spacer and one of the links, then through the length of the rung *(above)*. At the other end of the rung, push the bolt through the opposite link and the other small spacer, then attach the nut.
◆ Before tightening the assembly, rotate each spacer so that the round portion rests on the stool, and fit the chain links into the slots at each end of the rung.
◆ Fasten the chain to each spacer with the U-bolts supplied with the ladder *(inset)*.

3. Attaching the standoff rung.
◆ Hold a standoff spacer alongside one of the chains so that the center of the spacer's curved portion rests against the edge of the sill *(left)*. Mark with tape the link that lines up with the bolt hole in the spacer.
◆ Repeat for the other chain.
◆ Following the procedures in Step 2, assemble the spacers, standoff rung, and rung bolt, then fasten the chains to the standoff spacers with U-bolts.
◆ Pull up the ladder and store it in the box ready for use.

Coping with Everyday Hazards

Home is second only to the automobile as a dangerous place to be: Falls, poisonings, and other household accidents kill thousands of Americans and injure millions each year. Yet homeowners can prevent most mishaps by taking commonsense measures. Modest effort makes life easier for elderly or handicapped family members and keeps toddlers from tumbling down stairs or into a swimming pool.

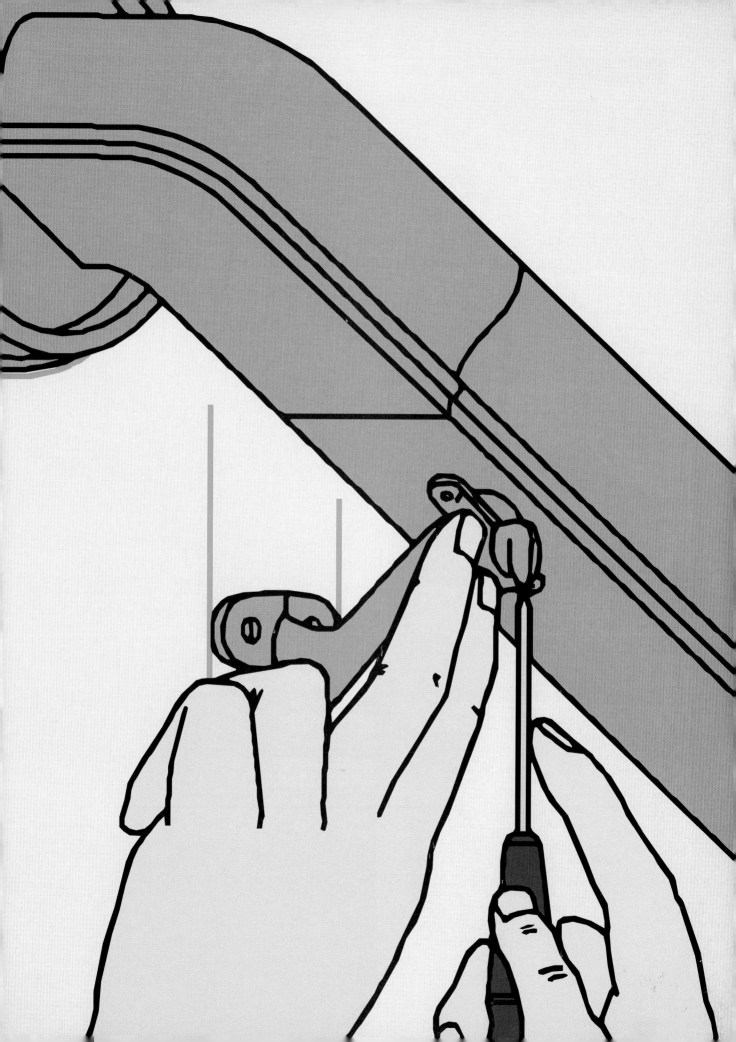

Should an electric, gas, or water emergency arise, you may need to respond quickly. Take time now to familiarize yourself with the utilities of your home, knowing where and how to shut off the electricity *(below)* and the main gas and water supplies *(opposite)*. Label all circuit breakers with the outlets and fixtures they serve, and tag the gas and water shutoff valves for easy identification.

If you are ever in doubt about your ability to handle a household emergency, do not hesitate to seek technical help before one occurs. The local gas, electricity, and water companies will answer any questions you may have.

ELECTRICITY

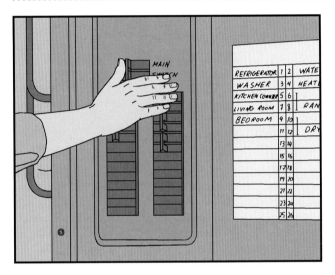

Shutting off power.

◆ Locate the main circuit breaker, typically a linked, double breaker of a breaker-type service panel installed above the other circuit breakers.
◆ Flip the main circuit breaker to OFF to interrupt power to the entire house.
◆ To restore electricity, flip the main circuit breaker to ON.

Individual circuit breakers are turned off and on in the same way. To map the circuits in your house or to check the accuracy of circuit-breaker labeling, switch breakers off one at a time, noting where power is lost.

⚠ **CAUTION** *If the area around the service panel is damp, stand on a dry board and wear rubber gloves and rubber boots. Use only one hand, and avoid touching any metal.*

Resetting a tripped circuit breaker.

◆ Allow the circuit breaker a minute or two to cool.
◆ Examine the device. If the switch has moved all the way to OFF *(left)*, simply return it to ON. To reset a breaker that trips to a middle position *(inset, top)*, push the toggle first to OFF *(inset, center)*, then to ON *(inset, bottom)*.
◆ If the breaker snaps off immediately after it is reset, disconnect one or two appliances and try again. If the breaker does not stay on, have an electrician inspect the panel.

GAS AND WATER

Turning off the main gas supply.

◆ Locate the main shutoff valve on the main gas supply pipe for the house. Usually it is found where the pipe enters the gas meter.

◆ Close the valve using pliers or an adjustable wrench, turning the handle perpendicular to the supply pipe *(right)*.

◆ To restore the gas supply, open the valve by turning the handle so that it is parallel to the supply pipe.

◆ Relight the pilot of each appliance following the manufacturer's instructions.

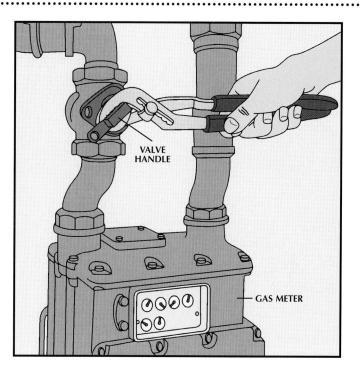

VALVE HANDLE

GAS METER

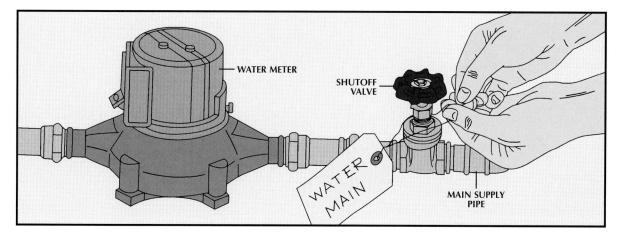

WATER METER

SHUTOFF VALVE

WATER MAIN

MAIN SUPPLY PIPE

Tagging the water shutoff valve.

Find the main shutoff valve on the main water-supply pipe. The valve is usually located indoors, often near the water meter. If you draw water from a well, look for the main shutoff valve near the pressure gauge or water pump. To help others find the valve in an emergency, tie a label, inscribed with indelible ink, onto the valve handle *(above)*.

A Plan for Lowering Radon Levels

Radon, a radioactive gas, results from the breakdown of uranium in water, rocks, and many types of soil. It typically rises through the earth and disperses harmlessly into the atmosphere, but it also passes through openings in a house's foundation and accumulates in living areas. If such concentrations grow too high, they can be dangerous; indeed, radon is a leading cause of lung cancer in the United States.

Test Kits: Since the gas is odorless, tasteless, and invisible, the only way to determine how much is in a house is to test for it. Homeowners can either call in a contractor to do this or administer one of the short-term test kits available at home-supply stores.

A kit consists of a radon collector, a seal, and a mailing container. Position the collector in a draft-free spot in your home's lowest lived-in level, and let it sit for 2 to 4 days. Then seal the collector and mail it to the laboratory specified by the manufacturer.

The lab will send a report outlining the amount of radon in your house. If the level is higher than 4 picocuries per liter—10 times the concentration in the outside air—administer a second test using either a short-term kit or one that remains in your home for 90 days. If the long-term test or the average of the two short-term tests equals or exceeds the initial reading, take steps to prevent the gas from entering your home.

Taking Action: Most of the techniques for reducing radon readings shown at right can be implemented at little cost in an afternoon. You need not take all of them to decrease your house's radon level; retest after each.

If levels remain high, consult an expert. You may require either the subslab ventilation system at right or a wall-suction system, which removes the radon that enters your home through the hollow spaces within a cinder block wall.

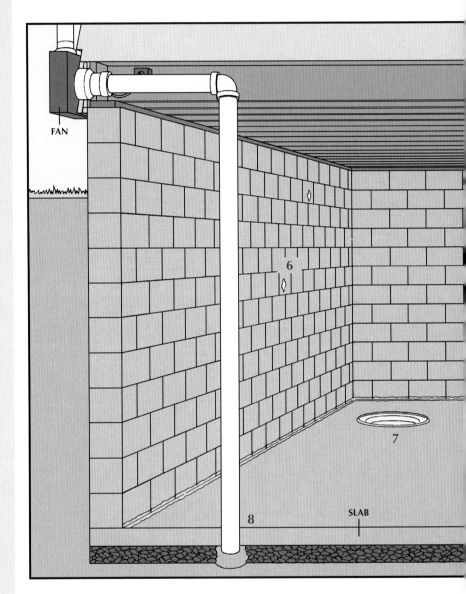

FAN

6

7

8   SLAB

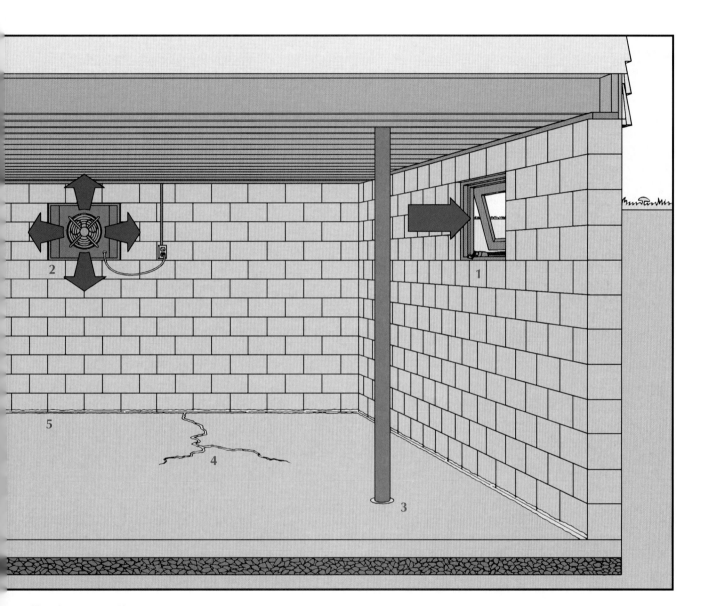

Effective remedies.

You can expel radon from a basement through a window (1) by mounting a small fan to blow air in through another window (2). To prevent more radon from entering, force caulking into gaps around pipes (3), cracks in the slab (4), and the joint between the walls and floor (5). In addition, inject urethane foam, available in aerosol cans, into wall fissures (6). Special plastic covers can be installed that seal the openings around some sump pumps. Cover an unused sump pit (7) with $\frac{1}{2}$-inch-thick acrylic plastic cut 2 inches larger than the width of the

opening. A bead of caulk under the cover fixes it to the floor; a second bead around the perimeter makes the cover radon-tight.

At this point you can remove the fan. If later retesting reveals that radon levels remain too high, a professional in radon abatement may have to create a path for the gas to bypass the interior. In the subslab ventilation system above (8), a fan mounted outside the house sucks air from under the foundation through a pipe and forces it up toward a vent at the roofline.

Fences to Secure a Yard

Many homeowners need fences to guard against accidents rather than intruders. Sturdy fences, for example, are required by most building codes to keep toddlers from tumbling into swimming pools. For a dog run, you may want an enclosure that can be put up and dismantled quickly.

Planning: For swimming pools, codes typically specify a fence 6 feet high, with a gate latch 4 feet off the ground. Depending on the locality, these fences can be made from chain link *(pages 8-14)* or from posts, rails, and pickets of traditional wood or maintenance-free vinyl.

For a wood fence, you can buy ready-made stockade panels, 8 feet wide, and nail them to the outside faces of 4-by-4 posts erected 8 feet apart *(opposite)*, or you can fasten individual boards to posts and rails as described on pages 105 to 107. Plan wood fences as you would a chain-link fence *(page 8)*, varying the post spacing as needed. For a post-and-rail fence, you can set the posts at any equal intervals up to 8 feet.

Dealing with Slopes: To build a fence with a level top on gently sloping ground, increase the posts' length to compensate for the slope of the terrain. On steeper slopes, the fence top should follow the contours *(pages 108-109)*. Build fence bottoms to clear the ground by no more than $1\frac{1}{2}$ inches to prevent children or large pets from crawling under.

Rules for Gates: On level ground, gates hinged on the side closer to a fence corner provide maximum access when opened. On steep slopes, gates should be hinged to the downhill post. Gate boards can be cut to match the slope, but the braces to which hinges are fastened should remain horizontal even if the rails on adjoining fence sections are not.

At the Lumberyard: Use pressure-treated lumber for wood fence and gate parts. Hot-dipped galvanized nails or aluminum ones prevent rust stains. In calculating post lengths, remember that they are sunk 32 inches belowground. To maximize the life of wood posts, buy matching post caps *(page 108, top)*.

 TOOLS

Shovel
Hammer
Carpenter's level
Water level
Folding ruler
Trowel
Combination square
Chalk line
Circular saw
Electric drill and
    wood bit

 **MATERIALS**

1 x 2 stakes and braces
4 x 4 posts
2 x 4 fence rails
1 x 8 gate bracing
Fence boards
Gravel
Ready-mix concrete
Galvanized nails ($1\frac{1}{2}$")
Gate latch
Gate hinges
Wood screws ($1\frac{1}{4}$"
    No. 10)
Post caps

 **SAFETY TIPS**

Wear safety goggles when nailing. Add a dust mask when you cut pressure-treated wood, and wash your hands after handling any fence parts that are pressure treated.

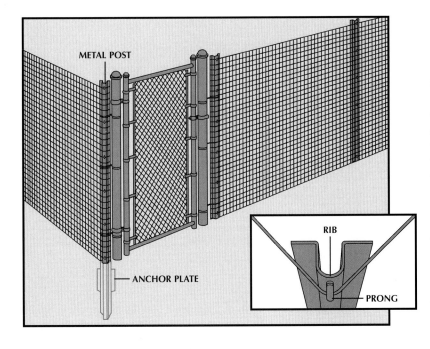

METAL POST

ANCHOR PLATE

RIB

PRONG

A wire-mesh enclosure.

Rust-resistant metal posts, firmly anchored by attached metal plates, support this wire-mesh fence at intervals of up to 10 feet. Lightweight wire mesh, preferably coated with vinyl to resist rust, is stretched taut by hand and hooked to metal prongs on the posts. Corner posts are placed at a 45-degree angle so that the wire can easily be stretched around the curved rib *(inset)*. A ready-made chain-link gate, complete with its own posts, is secured to the fence posts with tie wire to complete the installation.

SUPPORT STAKE

MARKER STAKE

1. Installing the first post.

◆ Mark the locations of fence posts and gateposts with 1-by-2 stakes.

◆ At the highest point along the fence line, dig a hole 1 foot wide and 3 feet deep.

◆ Drive two stakes at 45-degree angles on adjacent sides of the hole.

◆ Pour 4 inches of gravel into the hole and set the post in place. As a helper plumbs the post, nail 1-by-2 braces to the post and the stakes.

◆ Overfill the hole with a thick mixture of ready-mix concrete, tamp the concrete down into the hole, and trowel the excess concrete downward from the post to provide for water runoff.

2. Leveling the posts.

◆ Run a water level from the top of the first post to the stake at the lowest point along the fence line. Have a helper hold a folding ruler upright at the stake, fill the water level even with the top of the post, and have your helper read the height of the water at the stake.

◆ Cut a second post to this height plus 32 inches, and anchor it as in Step 1.

◆ Stretch a string between the tops of the two posts. At intermediate stakes, measure from the string to the ground to determine the heights of the other posts.

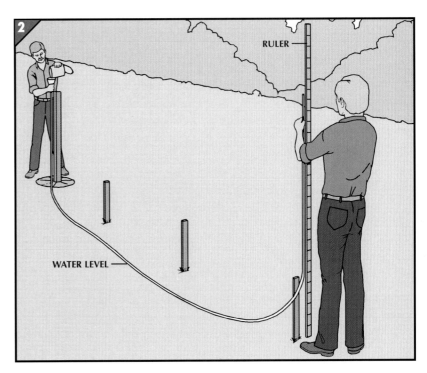

RULER

WATER LEVEL

UPPER RAIL MARK

STRING

LOWER RAIL MARK

3. Securing the rails.

◆ With a pencil and a combination square, mark a top rail position on the side of each post, 6 inches from the top.
◆ For the bottom rails, mark the side of the first post 6 inches above the ground. Use a water level to mark the other posts at the same height.
◆ Measure the distance between adjacent posts and cut pairs of 2-by-4 rails to fit.
◆ Align the upper edges of top rails and the lower edges of bottom rails with the rail marks. Hold the rails flush with the front face of the posts and secure them to the posts with galvanized nails or screws *(left)*. To avoid splitting the wood, drill pilot holes for screws; when toenailing, blunt the tips of the nails.

HARDWARE FOR HANGING RAILS

As an alternative to toenailing or screwing, fasten rails to posts with brackets called rail hangers. Made of galvanized steel, hangers are designed to support rails installed on edge, as shown in Step 3, above. The hangers are attached with special galvanized nails that come with them or are screwed to posts, and they can be mounted so that the rails are flush with one face of a post. (The brackets are thin enough that pickets can be nailed over them.) Use the nails supplied with the hangers to fasten the side and bottom flanges to the rails.

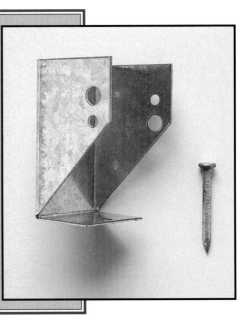

4. Attaching the fence boards.
◆ For each board, measure the distance from the string installed in Step 2 *(page 105)* to the ground. Rough-cut a 1-by-4 or 1-by-6 board to that length.
◆ Nail the board to the upper rail temporarily with the top of the board at the string *(left, top)*, making sure that the first board is plumb.
◆ Lay a length of 2-by-4 on the ground along the fence line and flush against the front of the fence board. With a pencil, mark the bottom of the board along the top of the 2-by-4 *(left, bottom)*.
◆ Remove the fence board and cut it along the mark. Reposition the board and fasten it to each rail with two $1\frac{1}{2}$-inch galvanized nails or screws.
◆ Butt each successive board against the last one installed, aligning the top with the string. When boards overlap posts, nail them at the same level as the rails.

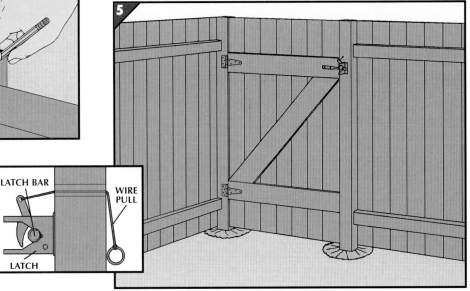

5. Building and hanging the gate.
◆ Cut fence boards for the gate *(Step 4)*. Also cut two 1-by-8 braces to the width of the gate opening.
◆ Lay the fence boards on a flat surface and screw the braces to them, 10 inches from the top and bottom. Cut a third brace to fit diagonally between the first two, and screw it in place.
◆ Set the gate on scraps of wood to center it in the fence opening, flush with the back of the hinging post. Mark the post at the top and bottom of each horizontal brace, remove the gate, and with

$1\frac{1}{4}$-inch-long No. 10 screws attach a hinge centered between each pair of marks. (Screws that come with most packaged hinges are too short.) Reposition the gate, mark the hinge locations on the braces, and screw the flange of each hinge to a brace.
◆ Nail a strip of 1-by-2 to the latch post as a gatestop. Position the stop so the gate closes flush with the back of the latch post.
◆ Install a latch bar on the upper brace, a latch on the post; to open the gate from outside, drill a hole through the post and tie a wire to the latch *(inset)*.

CAPS FOR FENCE POSTS

The tops of wood posts, even those made of pressure-treated lumber, should be covered to prevent warping or splitting caused by moisture penetrating the exposed end grain. Post caps *(right)*, made from rust-proof metal or pressure-treated wood, are available at lumberyards and building-supply stores. For a functional, streamlined appearance, push an aluminum cap *(lower left)* onto each post and secure it with a galvanized nail. To complement more decorative fence styles, choose a matching two-piece wood cap. Drill a $\frac{1}{2}$-inch pilot hole in the center of each post top. Push the screw of the top of the cap through the hole in the base, then thread the screw into the pilot hole.

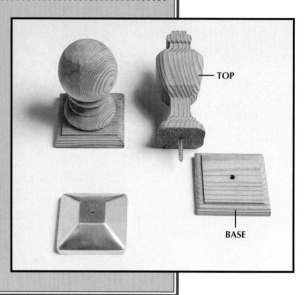

TOP

BASE

FENCES FOR STEEP SLOPES

Putting in rails at an angle.

◆ Install the posts *(page 105)* with their tops the same height aboveground.
◆ Mark the faces of the first and last posts 6 inches from the top and snap a chalk line between the marks.
◆ On each post, use a combination square to extend the chalk mark onto adjoining sides where rails will be attached.
◆ With a helper, align the top edges of an uncut length of rail with the marks on the sides of adjacent posts, and tack the rail temporarily to the posts.
◆ Mark the rail along the edges of the posts *(inset)*.
◆ Cut the rail at the marks and position it between posts, then toenail or screw it in place.
◆ For bottom rails, measure 6 inches up and repeat the top rail procedure.
◆ Mark the bottom of fence boards using a 2-by-4 *(page 107, Step 4)* and the top with a string stretched between post tops.

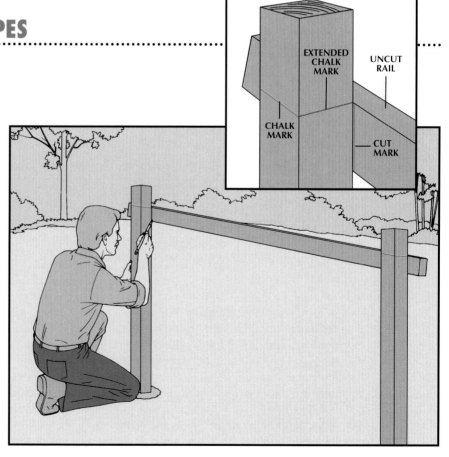

EXTENDED CHALK MARK

UNCUT RAIL

CHALK MARK

CUT MARK

A Clamp for Support

A wood clamp can substitute for a helper to hold one end of a fence rail in position for marking and fastening. Simply tighten the clamp snugly against a fence post about 4 inches beneath the positioning mark for the rail top. Adjust the clamp as necessary to bring the top of the rail even with the mark; then rest one rail end on the clamp while you work at the other end.

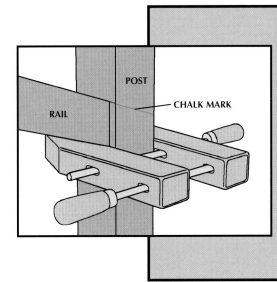

POST

CHALK MARK

RAIL

Hanging gates on slopes.
◆ Cut two rails of scrap 2-by-4, mitered to fit horizontally between the hinging post and the latch post. Toenail the rails in place, upper rail 6 inches from the top of the downhill post, lower rail 6 inches from the bottom of the uphill post.
◆ Cut boards for the gate as you would for a steep fence *(opposite)*, using the 2-by-4s for temporary support while you mark the boards for angle cuts.
◆ Lay the cut boards flat and add braces as shown on page 107, Step 5. Note both that the hinging post is downhill from the latch post so that the gate will not scrape the ground when opened and that the diagonal brace angles upward from the hinging post toward the latch post.
◆ Remove the temporary 2-by-4s between posts, hinge the gate, and install a gatestop and latch.

Though stairways are inherently hazardous, there are steps you can take to reduce the chance of a fall. If the stairs lack the vertical riser boards that close off the gaps between steps, for example, you can fashion some yourself and nail them to the boards that support the steps. And to prevent slips, cover the steps with nonskid wax or paint, low-pile carpeting, or rubber safety strips. On the pages that follow are two of the most useful techniques for increasing stair safety: tightening up a loose newel post—the large upright post at the base of the stairs that supports the railing—and installing a second handrail to the wall beside the stairs.

Securing Loose Posts: The method for strengthening a newel post depends on the stairway design. The presence of a bullnose, a rounded, ornamental bottom step that extends beyond the width of the staircase, allows you to tighten the newel from below the floor *(opposite, top)*. Otherwise, you must determine how the steps are held in place. Most older stairways support the steps with carriages, 2-inch boards at the sides of the staircase. The steps are nailed through their faces to the carriages, which are themselves nailed to boards called stringers, which in turn are nailed to floor joists at the top and bottom of the stairs. But in many newer stairways, the steps simply rest in notches cut into the stringers themselves.

Examine the ends of each step for nailheads or spots of wood putty covering set nailheads. These are the telltale signs that the steps are nailed to carriages, and that you can secure the newel post by screwing it to the outer carriage *(opposite, center)*. If you find no evidence of nailing, the steps are set directly into the stringers. In this case you must tighten the newel by either replacing its screws with new ones of larger diameter or adding 1-inch chair-leg braces *(opposite, bottom)*.

A Helping Handrail: Adding an extra handrail is advisable only for stairways at least 36 inches wide; it would make a less generous stairway too narrow. Choose handrail stock that measures no more than $2\frac{1}{4}$ inches across, since wider rails are difficult to grasp. In addition to a long, straight section of handrail the length of the staircase, buy two right-angle handrail sections called level quarter-turns and two wood end plates called rosettes. Hardware you'll need includes metal mounting brackets and rail bolts for joining the pieces.

With firm handholds in place, the stairs are as safe as possible for everyone except crawling or toddling children. To help protect them from a tumble down the stairs, close off the top of the staircase with an expanding gate *(page 115)*.

TOOLS

Combination square
Hammer
Electric drill
Spade or Forstner bits ($\frac{3}{8}$", $\frac{3}{4}$", 1")
Twist bits ($\frac{3}{32}$", $\frac{11}{64}$", $\frac{7}{32}$", $\frac{1}{4}$", $\frac{5}{16}$")
Chalk line

Socket wrench with $\frac{1}{2}$" socket
Electronic stud finder
Miter box
Saw
Framing square
Adjustable wrench
Nail set

MATERIALS

Nails
Wood dowels
Lag screws ($\frac{5}{16}$" x 3" and $\frac{5}{16}$" x 4") and washers
Chair-leg braces (1")
Wood glue
Handrail mounting brackets
Handrail
Handrail quarter-turns

Handrail rosettes
Rail bolts
Flat-head wood screws ($1\frac{1}{2}$" No. 8)
Finishing nails (2")
Wood filler
Child safety gate
Round-head wood screw (2")
Hollow-wall anchors

SAFETY TIPS

Wear goggles to protect your eyes when drilling and hammering.

STEADYING A LOOSE NEWEL POST

Reinforcing a post in a bullnose.

◆ Use a combination square to draw parallel lines across the step touching the newel. Then transfer the lines to the floor on each side of the bullnose *(right)*.
◆ Center a nail between each pair of marks on the floor and drive it through the flooring.
◆ Slide the combination square's ruler through the base and stand it on the floor with the edge of the ruler touching the nailhead. Measure from the ruler to the newel post and add one-half the post diameter.
◆ Working underneath the floor, use this measurement and the nail points to find the newel dowel's center.
◆ Drill a $\frac{7}{32}$-inch pilot and a $\frac{5}{16}$-inch shank hole through the flooring and into the end of the dowel for a $\frac{5}{16}$- by 3-inch lag screw, then drive the screw with a $\frac{1}{2}$-inch socket wrench.

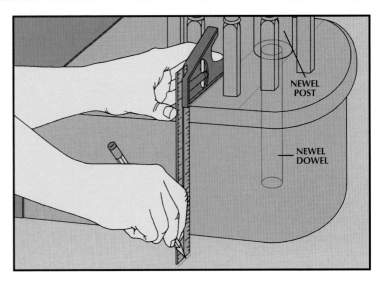

Bolting a newel to a carriage.

◆ At the center of the newel post, 4 inches above the floor, bore a countersink hole toward the carriage. Drill $\frac{3}{4}$ inch deep with a $\frac{3}{4}$-inch spade bit *(left)* or Forstner bit.
◆ Drill a $\frac{7}{32}$-inch pilot hole and a $\frac{5}{16}$-inch shank hole for a $\frac{5}{16}$- by 4-inch lag screw.
◆ Fit a washer onto the lag screw and drive it into the carriage with a socket wrench *(inset)*.
◆ Plug the countersink hole with a dowel.

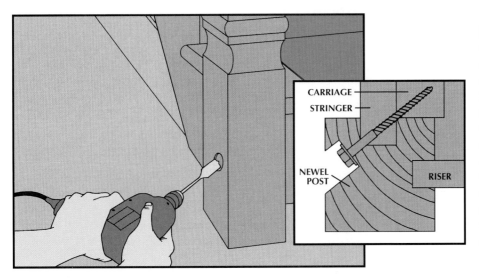

Bracing a newel post.

For greatest stability, brace as many sides of the post as possible.
◆ As a helper holds the post plumb, position a chair-leg brace on each side of the post and mark locations for screw holes.
◆ Drill pilot holes for the screws provided with the braces, angling the holes slightly away from the joint.
◆ Push the newel post from side to side and spread woodworking glue in any cracks that open between the post and the floor or bottom step.
◆ Screw the braces to the post, and allow the glue to set before using the stairs.

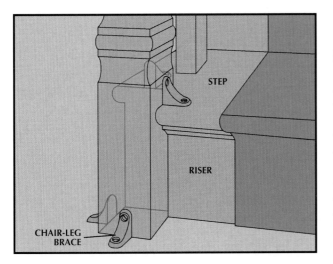

ADDING A HANDRAIL TO A STAIRWAY WALL

1. Positioning the brackets.
◆ Measure the vertical distance from the nosing of the bottom step to the underside of the existing handrail. Transfer the measurement, less the height of a handrail bracket, to the stairway wall above the bottom-step nosing and above the upper-landing nosing.
◆ With a helper, snap a chalk line between the marks *(right)*.
◆ Use an electronic stud finder to locate the studs at the top and bottom of the stairs and every second stud in between. Mark their widths on the wall along the chalked line.

NOSING

NOSING

RAIL SUPPORT

2. Securing brackets to the wall.
◆ Center a handrail bracket over each stud marked in the previous step, with the bracket's bottom edge at the chalked line. Mark the screw hole positions on the wall *(left)*.
◆ Drill pilot holes for the screws that come with the brackets *(page 27)*, and screw each bracket to the wall.
◆ Measure and note the distance from the center of the rail support to the wall.

3. Fitting the handrail.
◆ Lay a length of handrail stock on the stairs against the wall and mark it at the bottom-step and upper-landing nosings *(right)*.
◆ Cut through the stock at the marks, using a miter box to make square cuts.

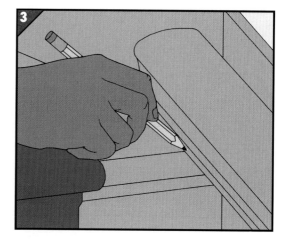

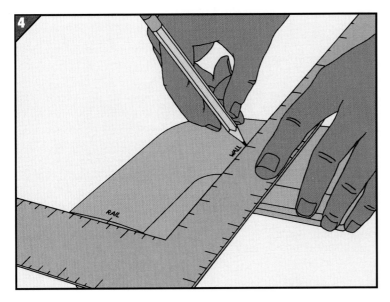

4. Trimming the quarter-turns.

◆ Mark a quarter-turn to identify the rail arm and wall arm.

◆ Subtract the thickness of a rosette, taken at its center, from the support-rail measurement made in Step 2.

◆ On one leg of a framing square, locate the mark that corresponds to this figure and align it with the center of the rail arm. Then draw a line across the wall arm along the other leg of the framing square *(left)*.

◆ Cut the wall arm at this line using a miter box, then trim 1 inch from the rail arm so the handrail does not extend too far beyond the staircase.

◆ Mark and trim the other quarter-turn in the same manner.

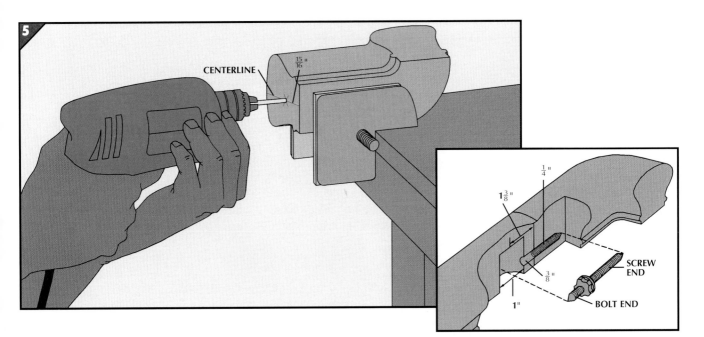

5. Joining the pieces.

Before you begin drilling any of the holes described in this step, secure the workpiece in a vise.

◆ Draw a vertical centerline on the rail end of each quarter-turn and mark a point on the line $\frac{15}{16}$ inch from the bottom.

◆ Make identical marks on each end of the handrail.

◆ Mark the bottom of the rail $1\frac{3}{8}$ inches from each end.

◆ Drill a $\frac{1}{4}$-inch hole $1\frac{7}{8}$ inches deep into each quarter-turn rail arm at the mark *(above)*.

◆ Drill a $\frac{3}{8}$-inch hole $1\frac{7}{8}$ inches deep at the points marked on each end of the handrail.

◆ Drill 1-inch holes $1\frac{1}{2}$ inches deep at the marks on the bottom of the rail.

◆ Run the notched nut and washer of a rail bolt onto the fastener *(inset)*.

◆ Use a wrench to drive the rail bolt's screw end into the quarter-turn.

◆ Remove the nut and washer and fit the bolt end of the fastener through the hole at the end of the rail. Replace the nut and washer through the 1-inch hole in the bottom of the rail and tighten the nut with a nail set.

◆ Fasten the other quarter-turn to the other end of the handrail following the same procedure.

◆ Fill the holes in the bottom of the rail with a wood plug.

6. Joining the rosettes and handrail.

◆ Outline the end of a quarter-turn on each rosette.

◆ Drill two $\frac{11}{64}$-inch shank holes through the rosettes within the rail outline *(right)*. Counterbore the holes on the backs of the rosettes.

◆ Mark the wall ends of the quarter-turns at the centers of the shank holes.

◆ Drill $\frac{3}{32}$-inch pilot holes into the end of each quarter-turn at the marks.

◆ Fasten the rosettes to the quarter-turns with $1\frac{1}{2}$-inch No. 8 flat-head wood screws.

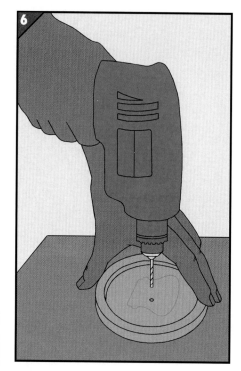

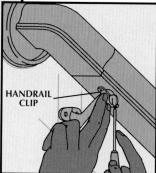

HANDRAIL CLIP

7. Installing the handrail.

◆ With a helper holding the handrail atop the brackets, mark the wall around the rosettes to establish the position of the rail *(left)*.

◆ Then place bracket clips over the handrail brackets and mark the locations of their screw holes on the rail *(inset)*.

◆ Drill pilot holes for the screws provided with the clips *(page 27)*, and screw the rail in place.

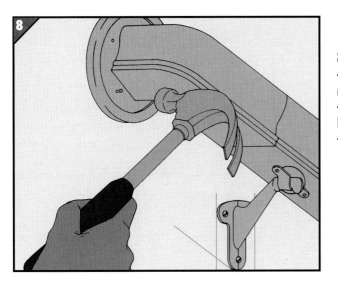

8. Fastening rosettes to the wall.
◆ Drill $\frac{3}{32}$-inch pilot holes through the rosettes.
◆ Drive 2-inch finishing nails through the holes into the wall, and set the nails.
◆ Conceal the nailheads with wood filler.

PROTECTING TODDLERS WITH A SAFETY GATE

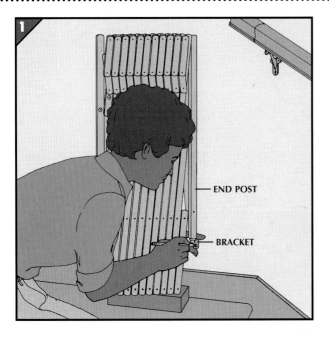

END POST

BRACKET

1. Attaching the gate.
◆ Set the gate on a scrap of 2-by-4 to keep it $1\frac{1}{2}$ inches above the landing.
◆ Fit a bracket to the bottom of the end post of the gate and set this post against the wall or newel. Then mark a hole on the wall or newel for a bracket fastener.
◆ Attach the bracket with a 2-inch wood screw *(page 27)* or a hollow-wall anchor.
◆ Set the gate in the bottom bracket and fit a bracket to the top of the end post. Mark a hole for the upper bracket and attach it with the gate in position.

2. Installing the catch.
If possible, mount the catch on the stairway side of the gate, where a child cannot easily reach it. Position the catch so the gate must be lifted for opening.
◆ Attach the catch to the wall using a wood screw or hollow-wall anchor. Place the slotted catch shown here with the open end of the slot facing up.
◆ Then insert the bolt through the hole in the gate post, slip it over the slot in the catch, and secure it with the wing nut provided.

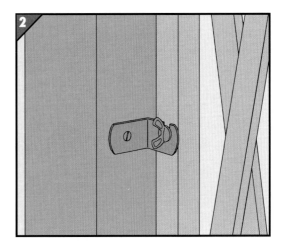

Safeguarding medicines, poisonous products, and dangerous utensils and tools is a necessity in a house with children. You can keep these items secure by installing a few inexpensive latches and locks on doors and cabinets.

Safety Latches: A variety of products for childproofing kitchen appliances are available at home-improvement centers, but with very young children, a simple homemade latch will keep the door of a refrigerator or other appliance closed *(opposite, bottom)*. A cabinet door can be kept safely shut with a concealed latch.

The model opposite will foil youngsters but open at the touch of an adult's finger.

Locks: A storage area sometimes may need a true lock to guard its contents. For sliding doors, a showcase lock *(below)*—the kind used in jewelry stores—is easy to install; it simply clamps into place. Swinging doors can be fitted with a hasp *(opposite, middle)* and a locking cam (rather than a separate padlock) that are screwed to the outside of the doors. A recessed drawer lock *(page 118)* can be installed with a minimum of time and effort.

TOOLS

Screwdriver
Tape measure

Electric drill
Spade bit
Wood chisel
Mallet

MATERIALS

Showcase lock
Cabinet latch
Hasp lock
Drawer lock

Fabric fastening
    tape
Double-sided foam
    adhesive tape
Dark lipstick

SAFETY TIPS

Protect your eyes with goggles when using an electric drill.

Attaching a showcase lock.

◆ With the doors open, slip the hook of the serrated lock bar around the edge of the inner door.
◆ Close the doors and slide the lock barrel over the bar until the barrel is flush with the edge of the outside door. The lock cannot be removed, nor the doors opened, until you unlock the barrel with a key.

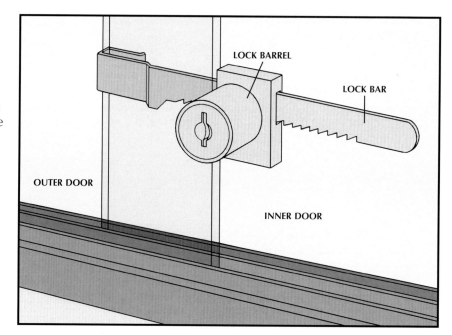

LOCK BARREL

LOCK BAR

OUTER DOOR

INNER DOOR

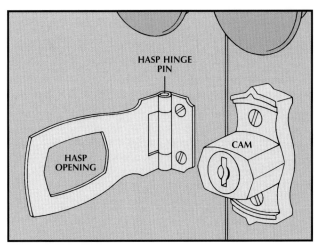

Childproofing a cabinet.

◆ Screw the catch inside the cabinet top no more than 1 inch from the front edge.

◆ Set the end of the latch shaft in the catch, swing the door onto the base of the shaft, and mark where the base meets the inside of the door.

◆ Fasten the base of the shaft to the door with screws. When the door is closed, the shaft will engage the catch *(inset);* to release it, open the door just wide enough to slip a finger over the shaft and push it down.

Installing a hasp lock.

◆ Measure the distance between the centers of the hasp hinge pin and the hasp opening, and mark the face of one cabinet door at a point that is one-half this distance from the edge of the door.

◆ Set the hasp against the door with its hinge pin centered over the mark.

◆ Mark the screw holes and attach the hasp to the door.

◆ Set the lock against the adjoining door and fold the hasp over the cam.

◆ Remove the hasp and mark the positions of the lock's screw holes, then fasten the lock to the door. To secure the hasp to the lock, turn the cam 90 degrees; open it with the key.

Securing an Appliance Door

A simple latch for an appliance door can be made from strips of fastening tape (commonly known by its trade name, Velcro) fixed to the door at a height beyond the reach of your child. With double-sided foam adhesive tape, fasten short strips of Velcro on the door and on the side of the appliance. Lay the fastening strip over them to keep the door secured.

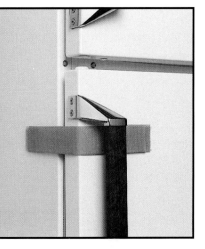

A RECESSED DRAWER LOCK

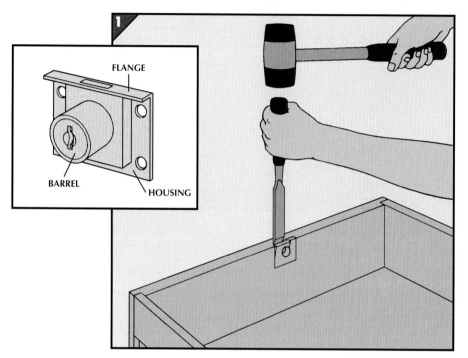

FLANGE

BARREL

HOUSING

1. Cutting the mortises.

◆ Measure the distance from the top of the lock flange to the center of the barrel, and mark this distance down from the top of the drawer.

◆ At the mark, drill a hole with a spade bit the size of the barrel and insert the barrel from inside the drawer.

◆ Mark the length of the flange on the drawer top and cut the flange mortise *(left)*.

◆ Reinsert the barrel, outline the housing, and cut the housing mortise.

◆ Screw the lock in place from inside the drawer.

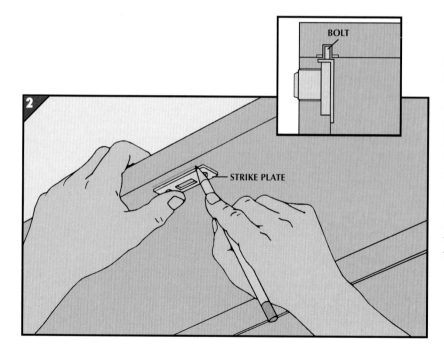

BOLT

STRIKE PLATE

2. Mounting the strike plate.

◆ Rub dark lipstick on the top of the lock bolt, close the drawer fully, and use the key to extend the bolt until it presses against the cabinet top.

◆ Remove the drawer, position the strike plate hole over the lipstick mark, and trace the outline of the plate and the hole *(left)*.

◆ Drill out as much wood as possible within the marks delineating the bolt hole—deep enough to seat the bolt fully *(inset)*—then chisel out the remainder.

◆ Cut the mortise for the strike plate, then screw the plate to the cabinet.

A little effort can pay big dividends in convenience for a family member who is elderly or one who uses a walker or wheelchair. Special hinges and doorknobs, for example, make it easier for a person in a wheelchair to pass through a doorway, while a kick plate prevents wheelchair footrests or walkers from scuffing the door *(below)*. In the bathroom, a variety of modifications can improve safety and accessibility *(pages 120-121)*.

Access from the Outdoors: A ramp transforms steps into a gentle incline for a wheelchair *(pages 121-123)*. Ramps and landings are adaptable to almost any entrance. For example, use a landing between two ramp sections to turn a corner or to double back to save space or reach a high doorway.

The ramp's slope must not exceed 1 inch of rise for every foot of length. At the door to the house, build a landing that is at least 6 feet long, and offset it a few inches toward the knob side of the door. Doing so gives more room for opening the door. The ideal width for both ramp and landing is $3\frac{1}{2}$ feet, wide enough for a wheelchair yet narrow enough for the person in the chair to grasp the railings.

Dealing with a Sidewalk: If a ramp's route is occupied wholly or in part by a concrete walk, you can let a few of the 4-by-4 posts that support it rest on the concrete; reinforce such posts by nailing 2-by-4 braces between them and adjacent posts.

Where most of the posts coincide with the sidewalk you must either widen the ramp or fix the posts to the walk with metal framing connectors that are secured by masonry anchors *(page 53)*.

TOOLS

Tape measure
Screwdriver
Electronic stud finder
Plumb line
Center punch
Electric drill
Drill bits (masonry, twist)
Posthole digger
Pickax
Circular saw
Hammer
Adjustable wrench
Water or line level

MATERIALS

Grab bars
Wood screws ($1\frac{1}{2}$", 3")
Machine screws and posts
Kick plate
Lever-type door handle
Masking tape
Toggle bolts ($\frac{3}{16}$")
Silicone caulk
String
Stakes
Prepackaged concrete
Pressure-treated lumber
Lag screws and washers ($\frac{1}{2}$" x $3\frac{1}{2}$")
Gravel
Galvanized nails ($3\frac{1}{2}$")
Pressure-treated plywood ($\frac{3}{4}$")
Marine deck paint

SAFETY TIPS

Protect your eyes with goggles while hammering, drilling, or sawing, and wear earplugs to mitigate the effects of the noise. Goggles are also advisable when using a pickax, to avoid injury from rock splinters. When cutting pressure-treated lumber, don a dust mask, and wash your hands thoroughly after handling the wood.

Helpful additions to a door.

Mount a grab bar 30 inches above the floor on the side of the door that swings against the doorframe. On a hollow-core door, fasten the bar with machine screws and screw posts running through the door *(photograph)*. A metal or plastic kick plate can be fastened to the door's bottom—for a hollow-core door, use anchors made for the purpose. To make the latch easier to open, replace the knob with a lever handle. Substituting standard hinges with the swing-clear variety allows the hinged edge of a door to move aside as the door is opened, effectively widening the doorway.

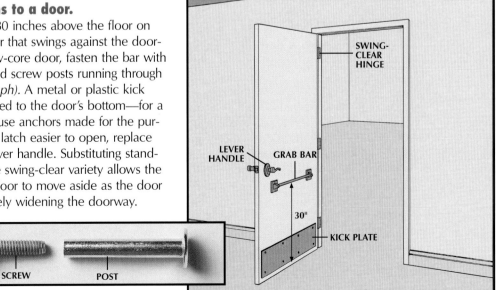

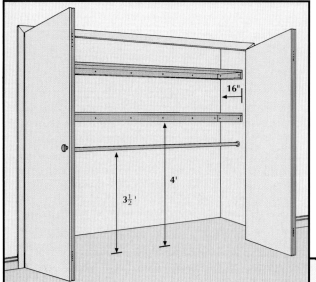

An accessible bathroom.

Grab bars installed on tub and shower walls *(below)* help prevent falls; for the toilet, buy a raised seat with support bars. A seat in the bathtub and a hand-held shower with a flexible hose mounted on a sliding bar simplify bathing. Tilt a wall mirror downward slightly by resting it on a strip of wood fastened to the wall and fitted with mirror clips, then adjust the length of the picture wire suspending the mirror. Replace a vanity with a sink that a wheelchair can roll under; be sure to insulate the hot-water pipe beneath it. Lever faucet handles, which are easy to grip, can be substituted for regular faucet handles.

A closet in reach of a wheelchair.

Move the closet pole to a level about $3\frac{1}{2}$ feet above the floor and install a shelf about 4 feet high and no more than 16 inches deep. Another, higher shelf converts the area above the lower shelf into storage space for an ambulatory person.

GRAB BARS FOR SHOWER AND BATH

1. Positioning the bar.

The grab bar shown here is designed so that each flange is secured by two 3-inch screws driven into a stud and by a toggle bolt next to the stud. (In new construction, double the studs in the unfinished wall and secure the bar with three screws in each stud.)

◆ On the wall above the tile, locate the studs using an electronic stud finder, then drop a plumb line from the center of each stud to the places you intend to anchor the bar.

◆ At those points, mark the width of the studs with masking tape and position the bar so that two of the holes in each flange lie on the tape.

◆ Mark all six flange-hole positions with a pencil.

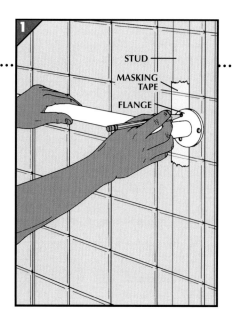

STUD

MASKING TAPE

FLANGE

2. Fastening the bar.

◆ Tap each pencil mark with a center punch or an awl to break the slick tile glaze, then drill through the tile at the holes. Use a $\frac{1}{2}$-inch masonry bit for the two toggle-bolt holes; for the wood screws, use a masonry bit slightly larger than the diameter of the screws.

◆ Drill pilot holes in the studs *(page 27)*, then remove the masking tape from the wall.

◆ Insert a $\frac{3}{16}$-inch toggle bolt into its hole on one of the bar's flanges, then fill the inside of the flange with silicone caulk.

◆ Push the toggle into its hole in the wall, then insert 3-inch wood screws into the remaining flange holes.

◆ Fit the bar to the wall and drive the screws in until they hold the bar loosely in place.

◆ Repeat with the second flange, then tighten the screws and toggle bolts and caulk around both flanges.

A RAMP FOR A WHEELCHAIR

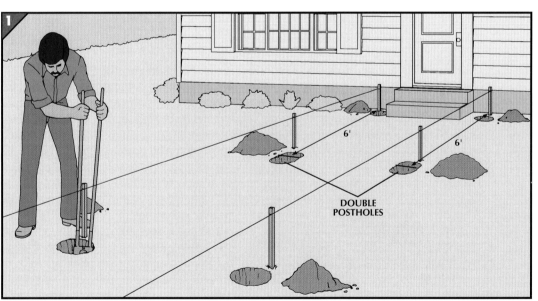

1. Laying out the ramp.

◆ As a guide for postholes, stretch two string lines perpendicular to the house—one line as close as possible to the hinged side of the door, the other 49 inches away on the opposite side of the steps.

◆ Inside the string lines on either side of the door, dig postholes 3$\frac{1}{2}$ feet deep and 1 foot wide.

◆ Dig the next set of holes 6 feet from the house. Make them 2 feet wide to hold two posts each. One supports the end of the 6-foot landing; the top of the ramp rests on the other.

◆ Dig the rest of the holes for single posts, spacing them evenly along the string lines. Place them no more than 8 feet apart.

◆ Pour 6 inches of concrete into each hole and let it cure for 24 hours.

◆ While a helper holds the posts plumb, alternately shovel and tamp earth into the holes, leaving unfilled the last foot of the two sets of holes farthest from the house.

2. Trenching for the ramp end.

◆ For the ramp to begin at ground level, excavate the pattern of trenches shown in the inset to partly bury the far end of the ramp framework.

◆ Dig trenches 4 inches wide starting just inside the end posts at a depth of 10 inches and sloping toward the house 1 inch per foot.

◆ Join these trenches with one dug 6 inches deep between the end posts and another 4 inches deep, 2 feet nearer the house.

◆ Pour 2 inches of gravel into the bottoms of the trenches.

END POST

END POST

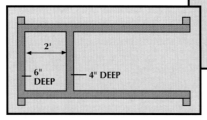

2'

6"
DEEP   4" DEEP

LANDING
CROSS BRACE

2 x 4
BLOCK

LANDING
POSTS

RAMP CROSS
BRACE

RAMP POST

3. Installing cross braces.

◆ With $\frac{1}{2}$- by $3\frac{1}{2}$-inch lag screws and washers, secure two 2-by-4 braces between the four landing posts. Position the tops of the braces $8\frac{1}{4}$ inches below the door threshold. If steps obstruct the brace nearer the house, screw 2-by-4 blocks inside the posts instead of cross braces.

◆ To support the top of the ramp, fasten a brace between the ramp posts $\frac{1}{4}$ inch lower than the landing brace *(left)*.

◆ Using a water level *(page 105)* or a string and a line level, mark the ramp posts at the height of the top of the ramp cross brace.

◆ For each foot of distance between posts, measure down 1 inch from the mark and draw another mark across the posts.

◆ Fasten braces on all but the last two sets of posts—position braces at the marks on the house side of the posts and $\frac{1}{4}$ inch lower on the opposite sides of the posts.

◆ On the next-to-last set of posts, screw 2-by-4 blocks inside the posts like the blocks next to the steps, but angled to match the slope of the ramp.

4. Assembling the platform frames.

◆ For the landing platform, cut 2-by-8 stringers 6 feet long and join them with 2-by-4 joists 39 inches long, spaced 2 feet apart *(right)*.

◆ Set the landing frame on its braces and nail it to all four posts with $3\frac{1}{2}$-inch galvanized nails.

◆ For each ramp section, set a 2-by-8 stringer on its braces. Mark the upper end along the post *(inset)*, and cut it along the angled line.

◆ Return the stringer to the braces so that the cut end touches the end of the landing stringer, then mark the upper and lower edges of the ramp stringer at the midpoint of the next ramp post. Cut between the marks and use the stringer as a template for a second stringer.

◆ Omitting end joists, nail 2-by-4 joists every 2 feet between the stringers.

◆ Construct the other ramp sections in the same manner, but for the last section of the ramp, cut the stringers flush with the last posts and install an end joist there. Use a 2-by-3 or 2-by-2 if a 2-by-4 joist will not

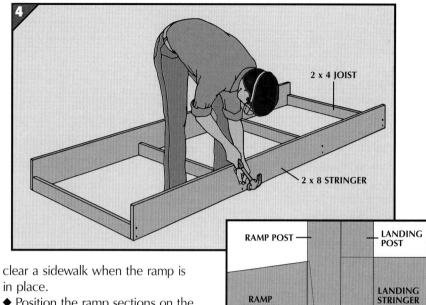

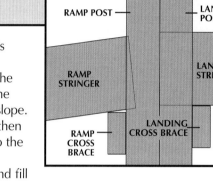

clear a sidewalk when the ramp is in place.

◆ Position the ramp sections on the braces, and adjust the gravel in the trenches to maintain the correct slope.

◆ Nail the stringers to the posts, then toenail the remaining end joists to the stringers and nail them together.

◆ Tamp earth around the posts and fill the trenches with gravel.

5. Installing the decking and rails.

◆ Deck the platforms with $\frac{3}{4}$-inch pressure-treated plywood. Make the joints fall on the joists, and leave a $\frac{1}{8}$-inch expansion gap at each joint.

◆ Nail 2-by-4 top rails to the posts 36 inches above the ramp *(left)*.

◆ Trim the posts at the tops of the rails, but sloped so the tops will shed water *(inset)*.

◆ Nail two more 2-by-4 rails, parallel to the top rails and spaced evenly between the top rails and the ramp.

◆ At a height convenient to the wheel-chair user, fasten a $1\frac{1}{2}$-inch, round hand-rail to the posts, securing the handrail brackets with $1\frac{1}{2}$-inch wood screws.

◆ Add a lever-type handle to the door *(page 119)*. If you have a screen door, remove the automatic closer.

◆ Allow the ramp to weather for 6 months, then coat the plywood with marine deck paint containing pumice; leave the rest of the wood unpainted.

While backyard swimming pools and spas can be sources of great enjoyment, they are potentially the most dangerous places around the house, especially for children.

There is no substitute for adult supervision when a pool is in use, but the area also must be made safe for those times when no one is around. Install layers of protection to prevent children from entering the pool area and to keep them out of the water should they get in, and alarms to alert you if they somehow fall into the water.

Lines of Defense: The first layer of protection is a fence. Check local laws or building codes for fencing requirements around a pool—almost all jurisdictions provide some sort of guidance—but as a minimum install a fence at least 6 feet high and built so that it is difficult to scale.

A pool safety cover helps to keep leaves and dirt out of the water, but its primary purpose is to prevent unauthorized access to the pool. The cover can be manually deployed or can be rolled out with the help of a key-operated electric motor. The model shown here hides the motor and spool beneath a bench. A solar cover, designed to keep a pool warm, is useless as a safety cover. It supports little weight and can trap a small child beneath it. If you have a solar cover, buy a pool alarm.

Don't scrimp on protection from within the house. Toddlers can wander out a door that is left ajar or unlocked, and a determined child can unlatch a window that opens onto the pool area.

Fencing.

As long as a pool fence is 6 feet or higher, it can be made of chain link (*page 8*) or wood (*page 104*). Build it with the posts and rails on the inside. Gates must close and latch themselves and have the latch mounted inside the gate.

Doors and windows.

Install self-closing and self-latching mechanisms on a regular door. For sliding glass doors, have a counterweight door closer and latch installed. A door alarm alerts you when the door is opened. Lock windows leading to the pool and install alarms (*page 62*).

Safety cover.

A pool cover should be able to support the weight of at least two adults and one child should anyone accidentally fall on it. Buy a model that lets rainwater pass through to avoid stagnant puddles and sagging in the cover. Because a cover for a spa or whirlpool is easily removed, it must be lockable.

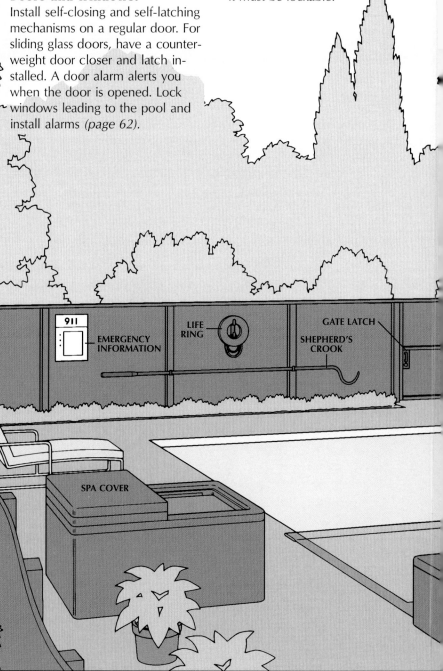

911
EMERGENCY INFORMATION

LIFE RING

GATE LATCH

SHEPHERD'S CROOK

SPA COVER

Pool alarm.

Place this device at the shallow end of the pool. Edge-mounted alarms *(photograph)* sound an alert both indoors and out at the slightest disturbance of the water. Floating models are less expensive but also less sensitive, and most blare a warning only outdoors.

Emergency information.

Post warnings, instructions for performing cardiopulmonary resuscitation (CPR), and emergency phone numbers in a prominent location. Consult organizations such as the Red Cross, YMCA, or a local recreation department for information on pool safety and CPR lessons.

Rescue equipment.

Hang a life ring with a rope at least as long as the pool's width and a shepherd's crook close to the pool. Keep them in good condition, and do not let children use them as toys.

Outdoor telephone.

A cordless or poolside telephone is essential in an emergency. It also lets adults speak on the phone without leaving children unattended in the pool. When the phone is not in use, keep it in a weatherproof container such as a plastic mailbox.

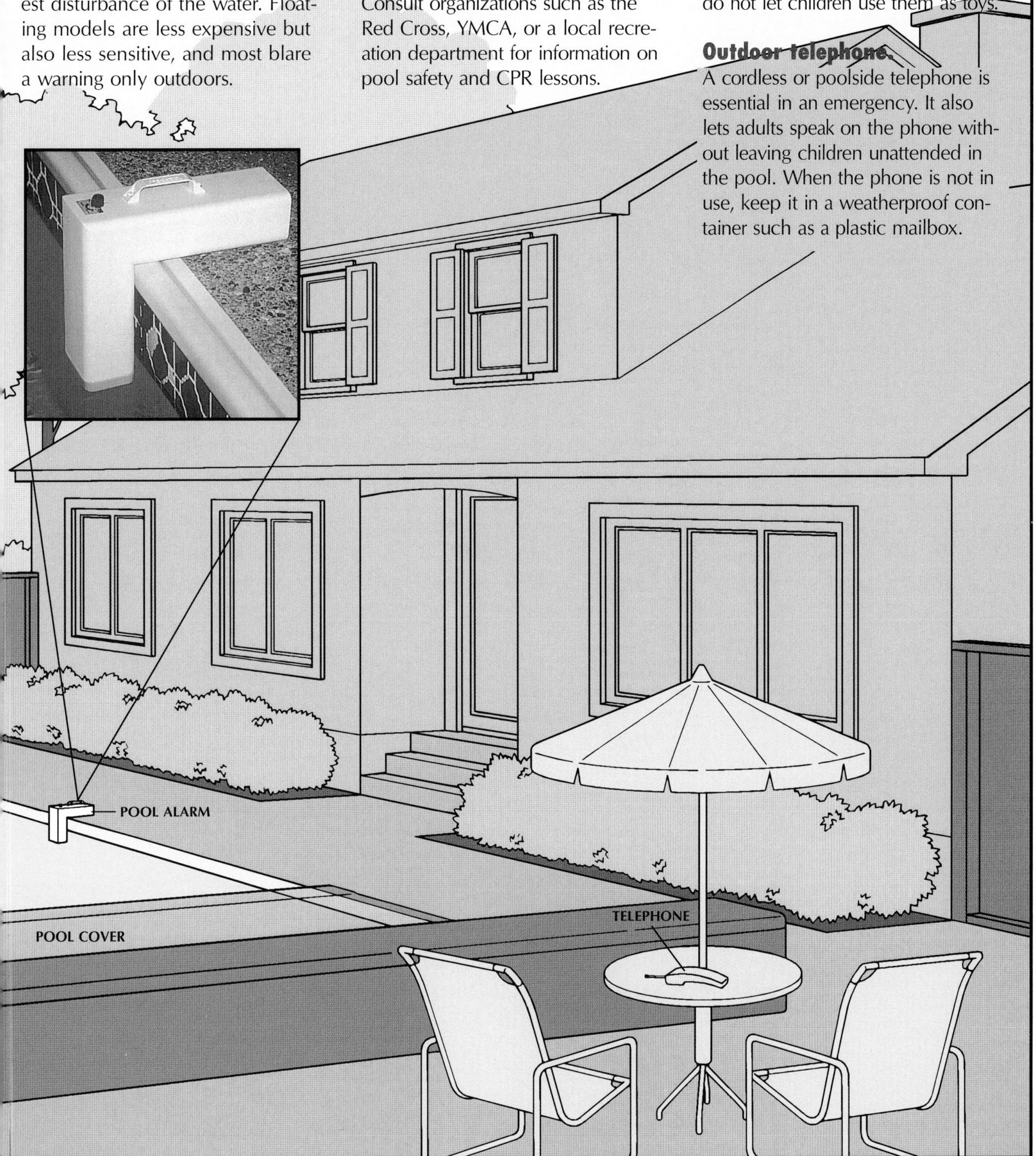

POOL ALARM

POOL COVER

TELEPHONE

Time-Life Books is a division of Time Life Inc.

PRESIDENT and CEO: John M. Fahey Jr.

TIME-LIFE BOOKS

MANAGING EDITOR: Roberta Conlan

Director of Design: Michael Hentges
Editorial Production Manager:
  Ellen Robling
Director of Operations: Eileen Bradley
Director of Photography and Research:
  John Conrad Weiser
Senior Editors: Russell B. Adams Jr.,
  Janet Cave, Lee Hassig, Robert
  Somerville, Henry Woodhead
Library: Louise D. Forstall

PRESIDENT: John D. Hall

*Vice President, Director of New Product
  Development:* Neil Kagan
*Associate Director, New Product Devel-
  opment:* Quentin S. McAndrew
Marketing Director: James Gillespie
Vice President, Book Production:
  Marjann Caldwell
Production Manager: Marlene Zack
Quality Assurance Manager: James King

HOME REPAIR AND IMPROVEMENT

SERIES EDITOR: Lee Hassig
Administrative Editor: Barbara Levitt

Editorial Staff for *Home Safety and Security*
Art Director: Mary Gasperetti
Picture Editor: Catherine Chase Tyson
Text Editor: Charles J. Hagner
Associate Editors/Research-Writing:
  Mark Galan, Tom Neven
Technical Art Assistant: Angela Miner
Copyeditor: Judith Klein
Picture Coordinator: Paige Henke
Editorial Assistant: Amy S. Crutchfield

Special Contributors: John Drummond
  (illustration); Jennifer Gearhart, Marvin
  Shultz, Eileen Wentland (digital illustration); George Constable, Brian McGinn,
  Eric Weissman (text); Mel Ingber (index).

Correspondents: Christine Hinze (London),
  Christina Lieberman (New York), Maria
  Vincenza Aloisi (Paris).

PICTURE CREDITS

Cover: Photograph, Renée Comet. Art,
  Peter J. Malamas/Totally Incorporated.

Illustrators: George Bell, Frederic F. Bigio
  from B-C Graphics, Roger C. Essley,
  Forte, Inc., Gerry Gallagher, Walter
  Hilmers Jr., Fred Holz, Judy Lineberger,
  John Massey, Peter McGinn, Joan
  McGurren, Whitman Studio.

Photographers: **End papers:** Renée Comet.
  27, 31: Renée Comet. **38:** Intelock/
  A Vista 2000, Inc. Company (NASDAQ:
  VIST). **53:** Renée Comet. **63:** Courtesy
  Samantha. **71, 72, 73, 78, 80, 83, 87:**
  Renée Comet. **89:** Jerry Pavia. **93, 106,
  108, 117, 119:** Renée Comet. **125:**
  Poolguard.

ACKNOWLEDGMENTS

Sandy Colon, Key Technology, Jonestown,
Pa.; Esther del Rosario, Washington, D.C.;
Mike Dietz, GMD Construction, Lisbon,
Md.; Silver Dohmen, Long Fence, Chantil-
ly, Va.; James H. Glazier, CML, Security
Plus Locksmiths, Mount Airy, Md.; Gary L.
Gross, Olde Towne School for Dogs,
Alexandria, Va.; Craig Hampton, Sheffield
Plastics, Sheffield, Mass.; Michael Haugen,
GE Silicones, Waterford, N.Y.; Steve
Hubick, Grinnell Fire Prevention Systems,
Elmhurst, Ill.; Jack Inderdohnen, Read
Plastics, Inc., Rockville, Md.; Roman
Ploskina, Therm-L-Matic Industries, Inc.,
Hatboro, Pa.; Julie Reynolds, National Fire
Protection Association, Quincy, Mass.;
Suzanne Mackenzie Stearns, National Spa
& Pool Institute, Alexandria, Va.; Alan P.
Zucchino, RadonAway, Ward Hill, Mass.

First printing. Printed in U.S.A.
Published simultaneously in Canada.
School and library distribution by Time-Life
Education, P.O. Box 85026, Richmond,
Virginia 23285-5026.

TIME-LIFE is a trademark of Time Warner
Inc. U.S.A.

**Library of Congress
Cataloging-in-Publication Data**
Home safety and security / by the editors
  of Time-Life Books.
p. cm. — (Home repair and improve-
  ment)
Rev. ed. of: Home security. 1979.
Includes index.
ISBN 0-7835-3899-5
1. Dwellings—Security measures—Ama-
  teurs' manuals. 2. Dwellings—Safety
  measures—Amateurs' manuals.
I. Time-Life Books. II. Home security.
  III. Series.
TH9745.D85T55 1996
643'.16—dc20   95-45807